CLASSIC
AFTER-DINNER
DRINKS

CLASSIC
AFTER-DINNER
DRINKS

SALVATORE CALABRESE

STERLING PUBLISHING CO., INC.
New York

Created by The BookMaker, London, U.K.
Creative Director: Lynn Bryan
U.S. Editor: Connie Novis
Designer: Jill Plank
Photography: All cocktails by James Duncan

Library of Congress Cataloging-in-Publication-Data Available

1 3 5 7 9 10 8 6 4 2

Published by Sterling Publishing Company, Inc.
387 Park Avenue South, New York, N.Y. 10016
© 1999 by Salvatore Calabrese
Distributed in Canada by Sterling Publishing
℅ Canadian Manda Group, One Atlantic Avenue, Suite 105
Toronto, Ontario, Canada M6K 3E7
Distributed in Australia by Capricorn Link (Australia) Pty Ltd.
P.O. Box 6651, Baulkham Hills, Business Centre, NSW 2153
Printed in Hong Kong
All rights reserved

Sterling ISBN 0-8069-5940-1

Contents

■

INTRODUCTION

I N MY FIRST BOOK, *CLASSIC COCKTAILS*, I TALKED ABOUT THE ART OF MIXING COCKTAILS BEING SIMILAR TO THE ART OF THEATER. ONE SETS THE STAGE FOR AN EVENING'S ENTERTAINMENT.

In this case, there is Act 1: arrival and an aperitif. Act 2: presentation of dinner with wine. Act 3: after dinner. To me, the bar after dinner is the final act of the evening and the bartender is one of the lead performers on this dimly lit stage.

I tasted my first adult after-dinner drink in 1971. It was a Brandy Alexander . . . creamy, intense, wonderful. I want to introduce you to the sensual pleasure of the after-dinner drink so that you too can have memories of special moments.

After-dinner drinks are more than a ritual at the end of a meal. Whether you drink port, cognac, or whiskey is of no importance; what matters is that you drink something strong, full of flavor, and with an exciting finish.

These "cocktails" fall into two categories: the true *digestif*, such as port, brandy, armagnac, and whisky and, secondly, the

Opposite
*A cover entitled '*Liqueurs by Lamplight*' from a 1908 edition of the French magazine,* Nos Loisirs. *An after-dinner flirtation sets the scene for romance.*

range of liqueurs such as Grand Marnier, Cointreau, and Bailey's Irish Cream.

A *digestif* helps to settle your digestive system—the word means "a substance that aids digestion." Imagine you have a fine glass of brandy in your hand; you swirl it around: you smell it, take the full floral bouquet up your nose—it makes you sing as you drink it. There is a sense of "Aaah" as you sink back and let go of the day's stresses. It, all the while, is working on your digestive system. You can drink any *digestif* on its own or in a combination, such as with brandy and port.

To others, an after-dinner drink must satisfy the need for something creamy and seductive, more a mixture of flavors than a distinctive single flavor. The liqueur is perfect. Some liqueurs have ingredients that can help the digestive system, such as crème de menthe, which contains a small percentage of peppermint.

To me, a good after-dinner drink is a refined combination of the bouquet, the aroma of each flavor, and the taste. When mixed together there should be one flavor.

The book is divided into six chapters: *Liquid & Luxurious: Brandy, Armagnac, & Cognac*, including a section on vintages and their rarity; *Smooth & Earthy: Malt Whisky; Classic Companion: The Cigar* (you can't write about after-dinner drinks without it);

Rich & Distinguished: Port; and *Lingering with Liqueurs.* The final chapter features over 100 after-dinner drinks, including ten future classics.

My journey here has led me along many liquid paths. Along the way I have had some great experiences—such as tasting a 1789 cognac. When I put glass to lip, and sipped this nectar, I thought I was in heaven.

There are many people to thank along the way, particularly the Rosewood Hotel Group, plus all of the liquor companies who have helped me with details for this book.

Hidden in every bottle is the magic of the elixir of life—your hopes and dreams need only a little encouragement.

Your good health!

Calabrese

CHAPTER ONE

LIQUID & LUXURIOUS:
BRANDY, ARMAGNAC & COGNAC

■

BRANDY IS A GENERIC TERM FOR A SPIRIT DISTILLED FROM THE JUICE, FRUIT, AND PULP OF ANY KIND OF FRUIT. IT CAN BE PRODUCED ANYWHERE IN THE WORLD.

The name comes from the Dutch word *brandewijn* ("burnt wine") and the creation of brandy was due almost entirely to the Dutch. From around 1570 until more than a century later the Dutch dominated European trade. Their demand for supplies of the new product, brandy, meant the French were obliged to change the way they shipped wine to Holland to be used as raw material in the distilleries, called *wijnbranders* ("wineburners").

A distilled spirit was cheaper to ship and the French wine was of a higher quality and was full of fruit flavor. The French began to

Opposite
Preparing an oak cask for the maturation process.

Opposite
Deliveries of
eaux-de-vie *from*
various areas of the
Charante region
used to arrive at a
distillery by horse
and cart in
decades past.

use the technique and equipment invented and introduced by the Dutch, particularly in the Charante region (see *Cognac*).

What we call brandy is made from grapes which are distilled, aged in oak barrels, and transferred to glass jars after maturation. The process is described in detail in the cognac section.

The age on a label provides details about the brandy inside. A two- to three-year-old is young; ten to 15 years old is good. Forty to 60 years old is of excellent quality.

Countries that produce brandy include Armenia, France, Germany, Italy, Mexico, Portugal, South Africa, Spain (the largest consumer of brandy in the world), and in the United States of America—the best Californian brandies from small producers are considered as good as the best products from Cognac.

GRAPPA AND MARC

Also called pomace brandy, these are "poor man's brandies." Marc is produced in France. The most well-known marcs are *Marc de Champagne* and *Marc de Bourgogne*. The *marc de champagne* has a delicate flavor, while the latter is aromatic. Grappa (see later in this section) is traditionally made in Italy. Both types of brandy are made from the remaining skins, husks, and stems of grapes that have been pressed to make wine.

TION DES EAUX-DE-VIE   J. & F. MARTELL - COGNAC

EAUX-DE-VIE—FRUIT BRANDIES

These are the spirits of other distilled fruits such as pears, apricots, plums, raspberries, and apples and are classified as *eaux-de-vie*. Calvados is a fruit brandy made from the mash of cider apples. Only apple brandy produced in the defined areas of the French provinces of Brittany, Normandy, and the state of Maine can be called calvados. The fermented mixture is double-distilled in a pot still and matured in oak casks for up to 25 years, gaining color from the wood. Applejack is an apple brandy made in New

England. The liquid is double-distilled in pot stills and is aged for at least two years.

Poire William is distilled from the Bartlett or Williams pear. The Germans call this *Birnenwasser*. Prunelle is a sloe brandy. Kirsch is a cherry brandy made from fermented cherries and brandy. Framboise (traditionally European but also made in California) is produced from fermented raspberries and slivovich is made from fermented plums. Each of these liqueurs is dry in style.

Grappa

The Italians have had a love affair with grappa for a long time. A spirit that is clean and raw in its taste, almost like firewater, it used to be seen as little more than the peasant's *digestif*. In the old days, it was common in northern Italy to see a man with a portable still traveling from village to village after the harvest, distilling each grower's pomace. His payment would be a proportion of distilled spirit, which he would then sell.

To make good grappa, fresh pomace should be taken to the distillery immediately after the "drawing off." There, water is added and the mixture is then fermented and distilled. It takes more than 26lbs (12 kilos) of the mixture to make nearly two pints (one liter).

Grappa is not necessarily aged, as such, but a few of the brands may have been matured in wooden casks for between two to four years. Production is mainly carried out in small-scale houses, and their products are sold in unique handblown glass bottles and flasks, often with labels drawn by hand. The best brands are expensive.

SERVING TIPS

It is usual to serve calvados, applejack, marc, and grappa at room temperature in a balloon glass after dinner. How much you pour in is always a personal matter. However, I would always pour a normal measure—about $1\frac{1}{2}$oz (5cl). Try not to fill the glass up.

Almost all good bars and restaurants in major cities and resorts serve regular brandy in a balloon glass, be it small, medium, or large. It is only the producers of cognac that prefer (and insist on) serving cognac in a tulip-shaped glass. I always fill the glass to about a quarter, leaving the drink a bit of space so that the aroma can come out. The warmth of the palm of the hand is enough to bring out the aromas.

Serve kirsch, slivovich, and framboise in a chilled shot or liqueur glass. Pour $1\frac{1}{2}$oz (5cl) into the glass and be careful not to fill it up. You can always have a second glass!

Opposite
Handmade bottles have always been a feature of grappa packaging. This is one of the beautiful bottles commissioned by Nonino for the 1996 Ue Monovitigno Picolit.

Armagnac

Dating back to 1461, armagnac is much older than cognac yet is not as well known since the market is dominated by cognac. The French know and promote this as the brandy of D'Artagnan, a swashbuckling hero of earlier times.

The *Phylloxera* virus also destroyed vines in Armagnac and these were gradually replanted, resulting in a 1909 declaration of an *appellation d'origine controlée* for brandy produced in the Armagnac region.

It is produced in Gascony in southwest France, in three areas: Bas Armagnac, which has acid, predominantly sandy soil; Ténarèze, which has chalky soil; and Haut Armagnac, where the soil is clay and chalk mixed with sand. The people of Armagnac learned the art of disilling from the Moors back in the 12th century.

Using the white wines from three main grape varieties—Ugni Blanc, Colombard, and Folle Blanche—the brandy has some similarities with its rival, cognac. The grapes are converted into wine in the traditional way. The wine is distilled by March 31 following harvesting, and distilled in a traditional Armagnac continuous still, invented by a Monsieur Verdier in the early 19th century. This distills to a lower strength and results in a more flavorful spirit. Some of the producers

Opposite

Some of the richness in color and flavor comes through the oak used for maturation of the eaux-de-vie *that are used for making armagnac.*

17

use a cognac-type pot still, requiring double-distillation. Unlike cognac, only a small amount of wine is double-distilled. The colorless brandy is piped from the still into Monlezun (the area's traditional wood) or Limousin oak casks. Most of the brands are blended, although there are single vintages dating back to the 1800s, and some single vineyard armagnacs.

Here you will find originality of style. These single-vineyard bottles bear the name of the distiller and each stage of the process has been handcrafted to ensure a top quality armagnac. Some may have been aged in oak grown on the estate over centuries, making the product unique.

Armagnac develops in the wood over a period of 20–40 years. Then it is transferred into glass demijohns to prevent it from spoiling.

It is sold in vintage years, based on the year of the harvest. In taste, armagnac is fuller, rounder, and slightly more earthy than cognac, with plenty of character, and a hint of plums, prunes, and raspberries on the bouquet. The label will usually tell you when the armagnac was distilled and how long it has been aged in oak.

Above
The rolling countryside of Armagnac in Gascony, southwest France.

Opposite
The most important ingredients of armagnac—grapes.

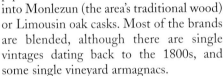

The difference between cognac and armagnac is this: imagine two exquisite fabrics in front of you. One is velvet, one is silk. You stroke both of them. The velvet is deep and rich, with lots of texture, and that is an armagnac. The silk is pure finesse and, for me, that is a cognac.

SALVATORE CALABRESE

INDICATIONS OF AGE AND QUALITY

The label on the bottle will feature one of the following statements:

***Three Star/V.S.
The name given by an armagnac producer to the youngest blend. A minimum of three years.

V.S.O.P., V.O., and Réserve
These mean Very Special (or Superior) Old Pale and indicate a quality armagnac. Sometimes abbreviated to V.O. A minimum of four years.

Napoléon, Vieille Réserve, X.O., and Extra
These are the finest products of each house. A minimum of five years.

Hors d'age
A minimum of ten years.

Opposite
The still is located at the heart of the production process.

TASTING & SERVING ARMAGNAC
To taste an armagnac you must use a glass that will allow the spirit to display its true characteristics. The tulip glass is the ideal

The French have always valued a certain Janneau-sait-quoi.

shape. Its form contains the aroma and allows it be released slowly during tasting.

Swirl the armagnac gently in the glass to release the true character of the bouquet. Fruity or floral aromas may be detected: dry chamomile, crushed grape, violet, and vanilla. This is called the "second nose." Armagnac really comes to life when it meets the palate. Here, flavors combine with aromas to reveal the character traits: roundness, sweetness, smoothness, refinement, lightness, and fieriness.

With practice, you can learn to identify the various characteristics and appreciate fully the taste and smell of an armagnac.

Serve in a tulip or brandy glass and bring the aromas out with the heat of your hand. It, like brandy and cognac, requires space to breathe for its delicacy to come to the fore.

Opposite
The clever double entendre works well as an advertising exercise for Janneau, one of the top brands of armagnac.

VINTAGE ARMAGNAC

There is a wide range of vintage armagnacs available today from more than a few houses. Some producers have ranges that date back as far as the late 1880s, verified by carbon dating techniques. Vintage armagnacs must be at least ten years old. Declared-age armagnacs, those that are aged for between 20 and 30 years, are reliably good.

COGNAC

Opposite

Early advertising images for cognac featured the concept of angels enjoying their share.

Driving from Cognac to Jarnac, with the sun deep red as it rises behind the misty hills, you see straight rows of grapevines planted from roadside to far horizon. It is then that you begin to understand the mystique that wafts past your nose every time you open a bottle of cognac.

To have visited Cognac is to have tasted serenity. Cognac is a vivacious spirit that has long been part of a family tradition—the after-dinner drink.

A SHORT HISTORY

It is brandy from the Charante region that is regarded as the classic brandy—cognac. The Saintonge vineyards were created in the third century when the Roman emperor Probus extended the privilege of owning vines and making wine to all Gauls.

The region's proximity to the ocean through the Charante River also made the town of Cognac a thriving trading center. Salt, called "white gold," was traded from here too. In the twelfth century, a wine-producing area called the Vignoble de Poitou was created. In the thirteenth century, the wines produced here were appreciated in countries located around the North Sea, transported there on Dutch ships that came to buy salt. The ships also collected the wines of the Champagne and

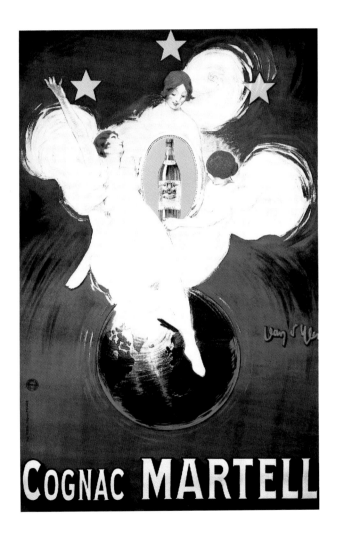

Borderies growing areas. It is not until the 16th century that there is a mention of the words *vin de Cognac* as cargo. By now the Dutch had established their own distilleries on the banks of the Charante, and the French followed suit, producing what we now call cognac.

The premier market for cognac was Great Britain. In 1678 an advertisement appeared in the *London Gazette* trumpeting the qualities of "cogniack brandy."

A French law of June 23, 1857 stated that trademark could be registered, thus protecting the quality of Cognac product and changing the relationship between French producers and English customers.

No longer was brandy shipped in nameless casks; each producer now bottled and labeled brandy under its own name. Hennessy, Martell, Delamain, Bisquit, Courvoisier, Camus, Otard, and Augier are the names of some of the families that were involved in cognac production.

As a result, the producers needed to identify what was in the bottle by age. The family legend has it that one of the Hennessys, Auguste, came up with the concept of a star rating. He devised a clever system whereby one star indicated a two-year-old brandy; two

In essence, a great cognac should be an invitation to pleasure.

ANON

Opposite
The rolling Cognac countryside.
Left
An old engraving of an early still. The system is more sophisticated today but works along the same principles.

stars indicated a four-year-old, and three stars a six-year-old. The term "old" meant more than six years old. The Hennessys did not register the system. A Monsieur De Laage did in 1868. Martell followed this system, too, in 1884.

What is Cognac?

Cognac must come from a small area of southwestern France—Charante and Charante Martime. This has been the law since 1909.

All cognacs are a blend of grapes from different zones, or *crus*, that spread out from the town of Cognac. Each area has a different aroma and flavor and it is this difference that gives each cognac its unique characteristic. A sniff of the glass reveals all the scents of the region.

Making cognac is the task of the master blender. Applying strict control throughout all of the processes, using experience and intuition, the master blender blends *eaux-de-vie* of different ages and *crus*, producing a cognac that will retain its personality throughout its life. In many houses the role is passed down through generations.

The grapes picked to make cognac belong exclusively to white varieties determined by decree. For regional *appellations*, the products must comply with certain rules:

Principal varieties (90% of plantation): late-maturing Ugni Blanc, Folle Blanche, and Colombard.

Additional varieties (10% maximum): Blanc Rame (Meslier Saint-Francois), Jurancon, Montils, Semillon, and Select.

Vinification has to be carried out using natural methods. The addition of sugar is outlawed, as is the use of a continuous press to press the grapes.

Maturing must take place in a cellar known as *Jaune d'Or* ("Golden Yellow") and only in oak casks from the Limousin or Troncais forests. The minimum period that it must be in the cask is 30 months.

Opposite
An impressive sight: row upon row of grapes planted in straight lines.
Above
The grapes that provide the best eaux-de-vie for cognac.

The finest grapes come from the Grande Champagne region, and a Grande Fine Champagne is made up exclusively from grapes grown in Grande Champagne. Then comes the Petite Champagne, and only those cognacs that contain a blend of spirits exclusively from both areas, with at least 50% of Grande Champagne, may legally be termed "Fine Champagne." Cognac from these two regions takes longer to mature and age than cognacs produced in the other regions of Borderies, Fins Bois, Bons Bois, and Bois Ordinaires. The majority of cognacs are the result of the harmonious blending of cognacs from several of these regions.

Other information printed on the label tells you about the age and quality of the liquid inside.

***Three Star/V.S.

Given to the blend in which the youngest *eau-de-vie* is four and a half years old.

V.S.O.P. or V.O.

These initials mean Very Special (or Superior) Old Pale and indicate a fine quality cognac that is ideal as an after-dinner drink. These initials are given where the youngest cognac is between four and a half and six years old. Sometimes the initials are abbreviated to V.O.

Napoléon, Grande Réserve, X.O., and Extra Vieille

These are the finest products; the youngest cognac is at least six and a half years old.

Generally speaking, the houses will use cognacs that are older than the minimum requirement. Those used in the prestigious labels may have been matured for between 20 to 40 years.

DEFINITIONS OF COGNAC TYPES

 *Cognac
 *Fine Cognac
 *Eau-de-vie de Cognac
 *Eau-de-vie des Charantes
 *Grande Champagne or Grande Fine Champagne: 100% Grande Champagne Cognacs
 *Petite Champagne or Petite Fine Champagne: 100% Petite Champagne Cognacs
 *Fine Champagne: Cognac blended exclusively from Grande and Petite Cognacs
 *Champagne with a minimum of 50% of Grande Champagne Cognacs
 *Borderies or Fines Borderies: 100% Borderies Cognacs
 *Fins Bois or Fine Fins Bois: 100% Fins Bois Cognacs
 *Bons Bois or Fine Bons Bois: 100% Bons Bois Cognacs

> *There are certain mysterious actions that we cannot define in the aging of the cognac.*
>
> MAURICE HENNESSY

The term "Fine" is authorized by a 1938 law to designate a Controlled Appellation Cognac. For example, a Grande Fine Champagne is a Controlled Appellation Grande Champagne Cognac containing 100% cognac from the Grande Champagne district.

The Fine Champagne Controlled Appellation is given to a cognac that is a blend exclusively of Grande and Petite Champagne Cognacs, with a minimum 50% of Grande Champagne.

THE PRODUCTION PROCESS

The harvest is mid-October. The grapes are pressed immediately in traditional horizontal plate presses or in pneumatic presses. The juice is then put to ferment. These two processes are closely supervised because they have the determining influence on the final quality of the *eau-de-vie*.

The wines obtained after three weeks' fermentation are perfect for distillation. When ready for sale, cognac must have a minimum pure alcohol content of 40%.

THE DISTILLATION

Alcohol is a product of the fermentation of the sugars found in fruit in the form of glucose or levulose. The alcohol is found with other components and therefore must

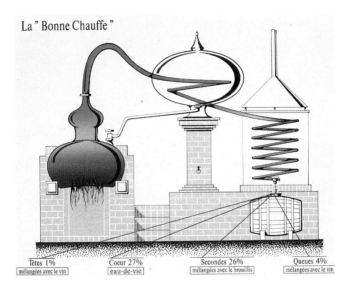

La " Bonne Chauffe "

| Têtes 1% | Coeur 27% | Secondes 26% | Queues 4% |
| mélangées avec le vin | eau-de-vie | mélangées avec le brouillis | mélangées avec le vin |

be isolated from them. This occurs during the distillation process.

Cognac is the result of the harvested white wines with high acidity and low alcohol being distilled in a specific, two-stage method:

In the still, the condensed vapors are sent back through the apparatus to be distilled a second time. The Charentais still is made of copper and features a shaped boiler heated with a naked flame and topped with a cowl shaped like a turban, an olive, or an onion. A swan-necked tube leads off this, becoming a condensed coil that passes through a cooling tank called "The Pipe."

Above

A fascinating illustration of the apparatus called "La Bonne Chauffe". This is the second distillation stage.

Unfiltered wine is put into the boiler and brought to a boil. Alcoholic vapors collect in the cowl, then enter the neck and pass into the coil. On contact with the coolant they condense and then drain away as the liquid called *brouillis*.

This slightly cloudy liquid is returned to the boiler for a second distillation, called *la bonne chauffe*.

The distiller then carries out *la coupe* (the cut). The vapors that arrive first have the highest alcohol content and are called the "heads". These are separated off. Next comes the "heart"—a clear spirit that will produce cognac. Finally, the distiller takes out the "tails." The heads and tails are redistilled with the next batch of *brouillis*. The success of the distilling cycle, which is approximately 24 hours, requires constant surveillance and it is here that the experience of the distiller comes to the fore. It is his or her technique that determines the final character of the cognac.

AGING

This takes place in casks or barrels that hold between 60 and 99 gallons (270 and 450 liters). The natural humidity of the cellars, with its influence on evaporation, is one of the determining factors in the maturation process.

The substances extracted by the cognac from the wood, called "dry extracts," give the cognac a color ranging from golden yellow to fiery brown. The transfer of the natural characteristics of the oak gradually

Opposite

The demands of the marketplace require modern equipment for reliable production. Here, a superb copper still is shown during the distillation process.

Opposite

Checking the quality of the cognac during its maturation in oak casks is a regular task of the master blender.

produces the flavor called *rancio* and develops the bouquet of the cognac.

Cellars used for storing the oldest cognacs are dark and damp and situated away from other cellars. Called *le Paradis*, here is where the cognac undergoes a natural evaporation. While the cognac is in the cask, absorbing the best of the oak and developing its flavor, it is still in contact with the air and gradually loses some of its alcoholic strength and its volume. The cellar masters call this "the Angel's share," which adds up to the equivalent of over 20 million bottles each year disappearing into thin air.

TASTING COGNAC

Tasting consists of analyzing the sensations aroused, identifying them, and classifying them so that you can distinguish their characteristics.

To professionally taste a cognac you must first ensure that you are using a glass that will allow the spirit to display its true characteristics. The tulip glass is the ideal shape. Its form allows the aroma to be contained and slowly released during tasting. The glass must also be fine enough to let the true color and the body of spirit to be viewed in its splendor.

Once the cognac is poured, put your nose near the glass to catch the *montant*—the aromas that instantly come from the glass.

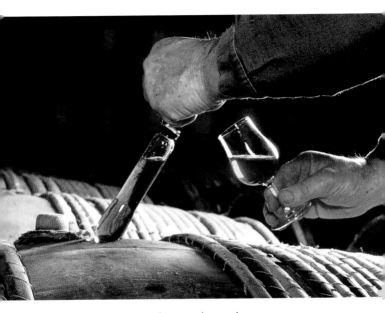

Swirl the cognac gently to release the character of the bouquet. Fruity or floral aromas may be found: dry chamomile, vine flower, vine cana, crushed grape, violet, and perhaps vanilla.

Cognac really comes to life when it meets the palate. Here, flavors combine with aromas to reveal the personality traits: roundness, sweetness, lightness, smoothness, refinement, fieryness, *rancio*, or harmony.

With practice, you can learn to identify the various characteristics and appreciate fully the taste and smell of a cognac.

GLOSSARY OF WORDS USED IN TASTING

Odor	all olfactory sensations smelled directly
Aroma	pleasant fragrance released by a drink
Bouquet	combination of aroma plus odor
Montant	first fragrance released from a cognac
Length	length of the intensity of the montant
Savor	sensations of taste on the tongue and palate
Taste	combination of savor plus aroma in the mouth
Flavor	combination of taste plus bouquet
Body	a spirit that is soft and smooth and rolls under the tongue
Rancio	term used in Charante to describe the flavor of cognac matured in oak casks, becoming increasingly intense over the years
Sweet, acidic, salty, bitter	the four flavors detected by the tongue

SERVING COGNAC

This powerful drink requires a powerful glass—when you are priviledged to sip the best cognac, you feel you have the world in your hand. Choose a crystal glass. The shape is important, as the section on tasting pointed out. The small, medium, and large balloon glasses are now out of fashion. The tulip glass is the one shape that will bring to you the best aspects of a cognac.

To those in the trade, the brandy balloon is called "the best liar in the trade" because of its shape. "It is like a mirror. When the aromas go up they hit the glass, which is too close, and come back to the middle of the glass, where they make a type of pot pourri before they go up in great gulps," explained one cognac master blender.

To him and other producers, the tulip glass shape is perfect. "You must hold the bottom of the glass to warm a cognac up. This action lets the aromas go up the glass—if they go up normally, the lightest at the beginning and the heavier at the end, then you have a lot of different smells and you enjoy it," explains Bernard Hine.

One point that all of the cognac producers spoken to for this book were adamant about is: Do not heat the cognac in a glass over a flame. The heat from your hand is enough to bring out the aromas, to humanize it.

"When you are given the (flame-warmed) glass you nearly burn your fingers, and when you put your nose on the glass the best has gone. The lightest smells are gone immediately as soon as you heat it up. You are given the second choice," remarks Hine.

The French believe that cognac does have a medicinal quality. It is a spirit, so therefore it will make the heart beat a little more quickly. It is also possible that a cognac may, after a heavy meal, help dilute fatty elements from your meal and make digestion easier.

Taking a cognac after dinner is best for your health because of this reason. Says Maurice Hennessy, "Members of my family who lived a long time had a glass of Hennessy before they went to sleep. In the house where my grandmother lived, in every bedroom was a little decanter of cognac and two glasses. It's a tradition."

A Liquid History

For many years I have collected vintage cognacs (I have over 300 bottles) and I also serve them in the bar at The Lanesborough in London. I was looking for that "special something" to serve my customers. I was keen on the idea that they could taste "liquid history"—sip a drink that was around when, for instance, Thomas Jefferson was president of the United States.

Cognac is the ideal drink. It is a noble distilled spirit and it doesn't age in the bottle. By chance, I came across a bottle of 1914 cognac, called "Ladies Vintage" because it was produced by women during the First World War years, when the men were away fighting. It was an excellent year and the cognac they produced has a wonderful flavor.

WHAT IS A VINTAGE COGNAC?

There are two kinds of vintage cognacs: those that are aged and bottled in the Cognac district, and those that have been aged and bottled in Great Britain. These are called "Early Landed." The vintage is the year that the grapes were harvested, and the quality of the wine is closely linked to the conditions of the soil and the climate prevailing that year in Charente.

Up to 1963, cognac houses were able to sell vintages. However, there were spurious bottles on the market that were difficult to authenticate. To protect consumers from fraudulent bottles, the Cognac Bureau came to an agreement with the producers to stop selling vintages. The only exception was for those cognacs called "Early Landed"—casks that had been shipped to Britain three years after distillation, and aged in damp, bonded warehouses under Customs & Excise control.

Since 1987 only brandies aged, bottled, and shipped under the control of French authorities are entitled to bear a vintage year on the label. For producers like Hine, Delamain, and A. E. Dor this was a small victory. Thomas Hine & Co. has always specialized in selecting, aging, and selling Grande Champagne Cognacs from a single vintage. Bernard Hine started to store his vintages back in the 1970s after proving from cellar records that whatever brandy was in certain casks or demijohns was put there many years ago and had since developed unhindered.

Their *paradis* has been locked by two keys—one held by the authorities, the other by Hine— since 1987. Hine's Grande Champagne 1948 has been kept in demijohns since 1974 and was bottled in 1987. A single bottle of Hine's 1914 reached the sum of

Opposite
A rare early label from the house of Thos. Hine & Co. is vastly different from the modern label, which is just typography.

Pancho Villa, when he was President of Mexico, reputedly said the only gringo word he liked was Hennessy.

Right
This brand of
cognac has been
promoted
unashamedly as
the one that
Napoléon drank
ever since a
drop of it
touched his lips.

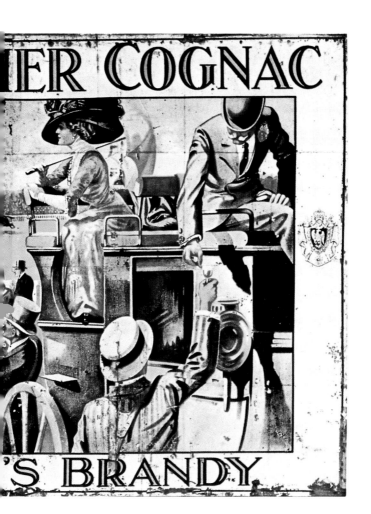

$1,000 in an auction ten years ago.

Hine explains, "We have put some away for the future. The vintage quantities are very small but they are beautiful to commemorate an event.

"Professionally we need them, because for us they are the memories of the past. If I don't put something aside, what is the next generation going to use? Looking at a span of 50 years, that's at least two generations, and the overlapping on each side concerns us. There is a tradition to be upheld."

Many of the vintage houses are creating a Millenium vintage. "The year 2000— that's something to celebrate in 20 or 30 years' time," remarks Hine.

Vintage cognacs are sold by auction houses such as Sotheby's and Christies and by private collectors and connoisseurs.

A recent sale of vintage cognac at Sotheby's London auction rooms revealed some very interesting prices. The bottle shown here is a 1789 cognac. It eventually sold for £12,000 (approximately $20,000).

Notes for collectors

* A vintage bottle is always handblown and the label will usually tell you the name of the house.
* The seal will be of wax, lead, or a chalky plaster.
* Always check the sales records of reputable auction houses to prove a bottle's authenticity.
* Be wary of some cognacs that have been kept in the bottle for a long time.

Quality can suffer if bottles have been stored on their side like wine. To be kept in good condition, a bottle of cognac must be kept upright in a cool and dry place.

Viscomte de Talleyrand, French Foreign Minister, was with his Prussian counterpart at the 1815 Vienna Conference. After dinner they both had a large measure of cognac. The Prussian took the glass, raised it and said, "Prost", and . . . bottoms up! Tallyrand was most offended and said, "My dear friend, that's not the way to appreciate a cognac. With a cognac you take the glass, you look at the color, you start to smell it, get an idea of it, and then put the glass back on the table, and only then do you start talking about it."

CHAPTER TWO

SMOOTH & EARTHY:
MALT WHISKY

T HIS CHAPTER DEALS ONLY WITH SINGLE-MALT
WHISKIES OF SCOTLAND AND IRELAND. AS AN
AFTER-DINNER DRINK, THE FLAVOR CANNOT BE
BEATEN, SAY WHISKY-LOVERS.

Opposite

*An 1890 bottle of
Glen Spey whisky.
Modern design may
have changed the
label, however, you
can be sure the
liquid inside is still
pretty much the
same as it was in
that year.*

The birthplace of single malts is Scotland.
The Irish, however, were the first to distill
and blend whisky. Intense rivalry exists
between these two nations. Each will have
to forgive me, an Italian, if I write about
them in the same chapter. To include all
the information on whiskies in this book
would be too large a task. Instead, I present
a snifter of the wonders of whisky.

Whisky-drinkers talk about this amber
nectar in poetic language, with words such
as "beautiful," "wonderful," "charismatic,"
"sensuality," and "exquisite pleasure"
slipping naturally off the tongue. To write
of whisky production is to tell of the misty

Highlands, of the smell of peat in the air on a rainy day, of illicit stills hidden from the Revenue men, of Bonnie Prince Charlie and his men sustained on *uisgebean*, of Irish public house bars famous not only for their whisky but for those writers (Dylan Thomas, for example) who drank in them.

Whisky has been accepted in our collective psyche as a man's drink; a seducer's tipple. So what is it about whisky that draws out the sentimentalist in us?

Scotland and Ireland are the major producers of whisky in Europe, and each country has its individual style. Canada, the U.S., and Australia also distill whisky, as does Japan.

The basic ingredients of whisky are barley and water, the latter being one of the key ingredients of flavor and aroma. Water varies from region to region in every country. Soft, hard, clear, or peaty are the main types.

SCOTLAND'S TREASURES

Distilling was established here in the 1400s and seems to have been used mainly for medicinal purposes. In 1505 the Guild of Surgeon

You use your nose for knowledge and your mouth for pleasure.

ANON

Barbers gained the exclusive right to distill the liquor. The spirit was raw and its taste was masked by herbal ingredients. Malt came to the fore as a choice of grain a century later.

The Scottish parliament taxed liquor in 1644. At that time many words had been used to describe what we now call Scotch, such as *Acqua vitae, uisg beatha,* and *usquebaugh* (corrupted to *usky* or *wusky*). It was not until 1755 that the venerable wordsmith, Dr. Samuel Johnson, entered the word "whisky" in his dictionary. (A note: to the Scotsman, it is whisky; to foreigners, it is Scotch.)

Without pure springwater, there would be no whisky. This is probably why some Scottish whisky distillers are located on the shores of deep freshwater lochs such as Loch Lomond and the River Spey. Scotland is divided into four whisky-producing regions: The Lowlands, Campbeltown, Islay, and The Highlands. Within each of these regions are several sub regions, such as the Orkneys Isles and the Isle of Skye. Each region has a characteristic "flavor" common to all of the whiskies produced within the zone. Those from the Highlands are generally smooth and smoky and are the most famous. Peat has more dominance in whiskies from the islands, often with a hint of seaweed. Malts from Islay are strikingly flavored. Yet of all the flavors, peat is most memorable.

Classic malt whiskies come from the Highlands and the islands, where both water from the granite hills, which makes it pure, and peat from the heather moors, have helped to create the originality of a whisky.

Single-malt whiskies are distilled in a pot still in single batches and must come from one distiller, and that distiller must be located within the boundaries of Scotland or Ireland. This was written in law in 1909.

"You can always tell the character of single malts. They are so individual and distinct. It's nice knowing it's a Speyside, an Orkney, or a Scapa or an Islay. Single malts stand on their flavor. Every one is different and has a combination of sweetness from the malted barley and a dryness from the smoky quality contributed by the peat," says Robert Hicks, master blender at Allied Distillers in Dumbarton.

HOW WHISKY IS MADE

The official definition of whisky describes "a spirit drink distilled from malt, with or without the use of additional cereals."

The basics of malt whisky production are as follows: barley is

Only a Sassenach puts the cork back in the bottle. A stalwart Scotsman throws the cork over his shoulder.

Opposite
This is one of a series of illustrated advertisements for Macallan whisky which uses humorous situations as themes.

soaked and left to ferment. When the starch from the barley turns to sugar, the barley is dried using a peat fire and fermentation stops. This adds a smoky aroma. The smokiness passes over to the spirit. The dried barley is called malt and is milled and mashed with hot water. This produces a sugary wort which ferments into a beer, which is then distilled twice in copper pot stills. A distillery features pairs of stills—the larger wash is used for the first distillation; the spirit still is used for the second. The condensate runs off the still and the center cut is collected. The first part has a nasty taste and is rejected, as is the last part.

Whisky must be aged in oak for a minimum of three years and, as in the case of cognac, most matures for longer. In the 19th and up to mid-20th century distillers used sherry casks from Spain. These imparted a rich hint of sherry flavor to the whisky. Since a lot of sherry is now imported in tanks, bourbon barrels are also used, giving a hint of wood to the flavor.

One of Ballantine's sales staff was the actor David Niven. His heart wasn't in the role, however, and he soon departed.

A classic malt whisky is distinctive and expensive—when malt is distilled, the angel's share is about 2% per year. When a whisky gets to be 30 years old at least 60% of what was put in the cask has been lost.

N A E
M A C A L L A N ,
N A E
F I S H

STORY IS TOLD of onald, a revered ghillie i a certain loch of our quaintance. ❖ It was a bad orning for trout, the water assy calm. ❖ Donald toiled l morning at the oars while s cargo of two London isinessmen caught nothing. lunchtime neared Donald gan to look forward to e lustrous sherry-gold pths of the bottle of HE MACALLAN MALT HISKY, the customary ward for a deserving illie ❖ But the otiose ssenachs had other ideas. "No fish, Donald," they ied "then no whisky." Donald quietly ate his nch at some remove. But the iron had entered s soul. The wind rose.

And all afternoon while every other boat was landing an amazing draught of trout, Donald rowed his clients slowly up and down the one unruffled stretch of water. ❖ When evening came he deposited his fishless clients on the bank and surveyed them gravely as they rifled through their treasuries of insult, goggling like the trout they had so signally failed to capture. ❖

"Nae Macallan" said Donald, at last *"Nae fish"* And rowed off into the gloaming. ❖

NUMBER
32

WHISKY AFTER DINNER

During the meal you have drunk perhaps an aperitif, a good white wine followed by a classic red, and possibly a dessert wine. Now it is time for the after-dinner drink. You require something that will cleanse the palate and excite the (probably tired) taste buds. A clean single malt fulfills those expectations. Yet one that is not too light. If you have eaten a heavy meal, a malt whisky such as a 10-year-old Islay— powerful and strong in flavor—is suitable as an after-dinner drink. If you want to try a 15-year-old, or even a 30-year-old, drink it after a lighter meal—perhaps after only three courses with no rich and creamy sauces. It is important to balance the whisky with the meal in the same way that you balance the wine with each course.

SERVING TIPS

After dinner, serve a single malt whisky in a fine, heavy-bottomed crystal glass. Pour it straight from the bottle. The whisky shines in the glass. Do not add ice. The equation is: ice=chill=less flavor. Also, do not warm the whisky. Its aromas are released the minute you pour it.

If you must, add a little still water, but not mineral water. This will bring out the flavors in the mouth. The burning sensation is from the alcohol, not from the flavors.

Opposite
A 1919 illustration shows a wake in progress for whisky at a New York hotel. This was a particularly tedious time for Americans —Prohibition!

Whisky-drinkers the world over have one thing in common: they like their drink bold and hearty. It is not a drink for wimps.

Cigars and malt whisky are not a perfect pairing. The harshness of the tobacco kills the flavors in the malt. However, this is a personal choice.

IRELAND'S TREASURES

It is generally thought that whiskey originated in Ireland. Irish monks, traveling through Europe toward the end of the Dark Ages, learned the art of distilling in the East and brought it home. The word "whiskey" (the Irish spell it this way) was supposedly first spoken by the English soldiers of Henry II when they invaded Ireland in the 1100s. By the 1500s this rich Irish product was gaining a market profile.

Irish whiskey has an oily palate, a perfumey note of the barley, and the roundness of malt flavor. Distillers use a combination of malt and "raw" barley in a pot still that is larger than those in Scotland. The minimum aging period is three years, although U.S. regulations require four years.

MAKING WHISKEY

The grain is crushed into a powder containing the husks called grist, then is added to hot water in a metal vessel called a mashtun. The mixture is then stirred by a mechanism. The natural sugars and other solubles dissolve into the water, which is then drained. This happens twice more, and then the remaining solids, called the draff, are removed. The water from the last mashing is reserved and used with the first water from the next mashing of fresh grist.

The liquid containing the dissolved sugars and grain, called the wort, is pumped into vessels called washbacks (or fermenters). Yeast is then added, which reacts with the sugars to make a beerlike substance. Once the reaction between the yeast and the substance has calmed, the liquid is pumped into the stills.

The number of times the wash is distilled—two or three times—differs from distillery to distillery, depending upon the type of whiskey. A single malt is usually matured in a sherry cask.

Irish malts are dried in closed kilns away from any influence of peat—maltsers do not use peat to fire the kiln. This means there is no smokiness in most Irish whiskies. They are also slightly smoother because of the third distillation.

SERVING IRISH WHISKEY

The same visual factors apply to Irish whiskey as do to Scotch. A fine crystal glass, heavy at the base, is ideal.

Irish whiskey is traditionally served straight, with a small jug of still water for the consumer to dilute it if preferred.

CHAPTER THREE

CLASSIC COMPANION: THE CIGAR

THE AFTER-DINNER DRINK AND THE CIGAR ARE SYNONYMOUS WITH PLEASURE, LUXURY, RELAXATION, AND POWER. AS AN APHRODISIAC, THERE IS NOTHING QUITE LIKE IT.

The cigar is unique in having all of the above magical qualities attributed to it before it has even left the field. Once it is lit and in the hands of a tycoon it is truly imbued with magical qualities.

The rediscovered cigar culture has become a social phenomenon. Far from being seen as a status symbol of the middle-aged, the cigar is now seen as hip by a younger generation. A Havana cigar is by far the most desired cigar in the world.

"Tobacco," "earthy," "golden," "nutty," "smokey flavors"—these words roll off the tongue in a conversation about a cigar in the same way that they do when an armagnac, a cognac, or a whisky is discussed.

Opposite
A cigar from the Dominican Republic burns in an ashtray. Note the cigar band is still wrapped around the body of the cigar.

TWO THINGS TO KNOW ABOUT A CIGAR

The quality of a cigar is the result of the type and quality of leaves used in its construction.

The wrapper leaf is important—it sets the appearance and aroma of the cigar. The best cigars have wrapper leaves made from the Corojos plant.

Native peoples of North and Central America knew all about the pleasure of tobacco and cigars way before Hollywood producer Darryl F. Zanuck or statesman Sir Winston Churchill did. The Havana cigar arrived in America in 1762 when an American general returned to Connecticut from Cuba with a selection of Havana cigars.

Cigar smoking became a fashion in 19th-century Europe to the extent that smoking rooms in private clubs and refined hotels, along with smoking cars on trains, were required to protect those who did not indulge from the smog of thick cigar smoke.

To Cubans, cigar-making was (still is) a way of life. Fidel Castro's declaration of independence from Spain resulted in a U.S. Government embargo in 1962, which stated that Cuban cigars could not be imported into U.S.. When Cuban businesses were nationalized, many of the cigar families departed to set up factories in other countries.

Cigars are made in the Vuelta Abajo area of the Pinar del Rio province, Cuba, Dominican Republic, Miami in the U.S.,

Honduras, Mexico, Jamaica, Nicaragua, Ecuador, Brazil, Germany, Indonesia, the Netherlands, Switzerland, and Cameroon.

THE HANDMADE CIGAR

The tobacco plant's leaves are all useful—some leaves are binders, others are fillers and wrappers. Cigars are classified as having mild, medium, or full flavor.

The leaves are the key to flavor. Once the leaves are picked by hand, they are cured in a barn on the plantation. The temperature and humidity are controlled. The leaves are hung on horizontal poles to let air circulate.

The next step takes place in fermentation houses. The bundles of leaves are piled high and covered with sheets of jute. Heat builds up over the time the bundles are left under cover and the leaves become a regular color.

Then, the bundles are separated and the leaves cooled before being taken to the sorting house. Here they are graded by texture, color, and size. This task is done by women who flatten the choice leaves on boards ready to be returned to the fermentation house. The leaves are stacked and a second fermentation occurs. The result is a less acidic tobacco that contains less tar and nicotine than cigarette tobacco.

THE LARGEST CIGAR IN THE WORLD

Before the Second World War Henry Clay made a cigar, Koh-i-Noor, for a maharaja.

It measured 18 inches long, with a 47 gauge ring size.

The word "cigar" has its origins in Mayan language: sikar *is their word for smoking.*

WRAPPERS

The wrapper, called a capa, creates the appearance—it should have no protruding veins. There is a range of colors:

Claro (also called natural): The classic color of a mild cigar, this is a pale brown.

Double claro: A green/brown color—the result of having been picked before maturity and force-dried.

Colorado claro: A medium brown.

Colorado: A russet brown.

Colorado maduro: A rich dark brown.

Maduro: A very dark brown.

Oscuro: More black than brown.

FILLERS

These consist of separate leaves folded lengthwise so as to draw air when the cigar is lit. They usually have three types of leaves: *ligero* in the center, *seco*, and *volado*.

BINDERS

Called a *capote*, this binds the cigar and is generally strong.

ROLLING A CIGAR

Contrary to the legend, all handmade cigars are not rolled between the slender thighs of a Cuban virgin. Much skill is involved in rolling a cigar. The filler must be distributed evenly to allow the cigar to draw properly. The blended fillers are placed in a wooden mold and pressed and the extra is trimmed. A wrapper leaf is chosen, then the pressed filler is placed at an angle on the wrapper, which is stretched and wound around the binder. The cigar is then rolled with a flat steel blade to ensure it is even along the length. The cap is made from a spare piece of wrapper and then put in place.

IS IT GENUINE?

How can you tell if a Havana cigar is genuinely made by hand? Look for the words *Totalmente a Mano* and *Hecho en Cuba* stamped on the underside of the box, plus a factory code and a *Cubatabaco* logo (pre-1994) or *Habanos s.a.* (post-1994).

You can buy Havanas in most parts of the world, except the U.S.. Be vigilant. It is best to buy them in a box or, if you have to buy single cigars, buy only from a reputable store or bar. Forty percent of the Havanas available are not genuine.

SEEN WITH
A CIGAR

Harvey Keitel (who could forget him in Smoke*!)*
Groucho Marx
John Quincy Adams
Ulysess Grant
Edward VII
Fidel Castro
Sir Winston Churchill
Arnold Schwarzenegger
William Jefferson Clinton
Sylvester Stallone
Bob Hoskins
Marvin Shanken
Orson Welles
Gabriel Byrne
Edward G. Robinson
Michael Caine
Clint Eastwood
George Burns
Charlie Chaplin

SIZES

Opposite
A bunch of tobacco leaves waiting to be made into a cigar.

There are many sizes. Makers such as Davidoff offer 19 sizes; Cohiba and Montecristo make 11 sizes. Cuba manufactures 69 sizes! Partagas produce 40.

Nor are cigars of a standard girth. Makers talk of a cigar's ring gauge in $1/64$ths of an inch. For instance, a 52 would be $52/64$ths of an inch. Most are between nine inches down to four and a half long.

CUTTING THE CIGAR

Try to leave at least $1/8$ inch of the cap—do not cut below the cap area. Cut it evenly. There are a variety of cigar-cutters available ranging from single- and double-blade guillotine types to elegant scissors.

THE BAND

This was introduced by Gustave Bock in a move to identify his brand over others. It also has a practical use—it protects the fingers from becoming stained. Whether you smoke a cigar with it on or off is a matter of personal style. You can ruin a wrapper if you take the band off while the cigar is unlit.

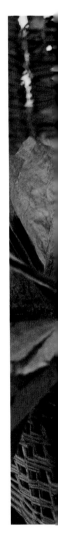

MACHINE-MADE CIGARS

A machine-made cigar is, by definition, different from a handmade cigar in one major way: in a machine-made cigar, its filler is made from small pieces of leaf. The way a machine-made cigar draws is nowhere near as even and slow as a handmade cigar.

WHICH CIGAR TO SMOKE WITH WHICH DRINK?

With cognac: a full-flavored Cuban cigar may overpower the flavor of a young cognac. Experienced smokers recommend a V.S.O.P. cognac with a milder cigar. A Fine Grande Champagne is good with most cigars, as is a Napoléon.

Several cognac-makers have created a cognac suited to the palate of those who smoke cigars. Hine's Cigar Reserve Cognac is somewhere between a V.S.O.P. and an X.O.—a drink with body to match the strength of a cigar.

Some port manufacturers do not think you should smoke a cigar with port since it can ruin the flavor. The same comment came from some of the malt whisky-makers. It is entirely up to you whether you smoke a cigar while enjoying an after-dinner drink.

Opposite

A collection of cigars in metal cylinders is displayed on top of a large tobacco leaf. Butane lighters are best to use for lighting cigars.

CHAPTER FOUR

RICH & DISTINGUISHED:
PORT

∎

PORT REMAINS A POPULAR AFTER-DINNER DRINK.
THE RICHNESS OF ITS COLOR, AND ITS
SMOOTHNESS, CAN BRING BOTH DELICACY
AND STRENGTH TO THE JADED PALATE.

Opposite
Sensual imagery in
a 1926 poster for
Sandeman's port
was created by
French artist
Jean D'Ylen.

Port used to be thought of as an old man's drink. However, its image has changed over the past two decades.

Traditionally, port is made with wine grown in the region of Douro east of Oporto in Portugal. In 1756 the Marques de Pombal, then prime minister of Portugal, set out the geographical location of the Douro District which was then recognized as the *Appellation d'Origine*. Surrounded by mountains, the region's combination of soil, climate, and vine varieties contribute to port's characteristics. Its residents are dedicated to making port. When visiting the numerous *quintas* (vineyard estates) and talking to the people

behind the labels, their passion for port quickly becomes evident. Also, the difference between port and port wine is verbally defined: they speak of wood-aged ports such as ruby and tawny as port; they refer to vintage ports as port wine.

The name "port" or "port wine" is an abbreviation of the translation of the Portuguese name *Vinho do Porto*.

Port's history is closely linked to Britain. It was in the 1800s that the British turned to Portugal as an inexpensive source of red table wine. It often arrived in Britain in poor condition, however, so British merchants in Oporto added brandy to the wine to help it travel well.

The tradition of passing the port bottle from the right to to your left is also British. This ritual is taken seriously by port drinkers, to the extent that small wheels have been attached to silver coasters to ensure a smooth passage around the table. Fail to pass the port and your reputation could be ruined!

The *Phylloxera* germ, which attacks the base of the vine, struck the vineyard estates in the Douro Valley. From 1868, the port wine producers were devastated by the bug. However, 1884 was a turning point. Only one area of the Quinta do Noval vineyard estate—called the Naçional—survived the outbreak. Geographically, it is located higher up in the vineyard. Quinta do Noval's Naçional is made from this original root stock and this is why it is more expensive than some of the other ports.

Types of Port

There are two types of port: wood-aged and bottle-aged.

WOOD-AGED port wine includes styles such as white (drunk as an aperitif), ruby, tawny, vintage character, and late-bottled vintage, as well as old tawnies and vintage-dated tawnies. Each of these is blended from port wine that has been aged in oak wood casks and treated to remove any solids before bottling.

Ruby is a blend of young, fruity ports bottled after spending three years in wood. The wine has a dark ruby color (hence the name) and a full fruit aroma.

Vintage Character port is a blended port bottled after four years and must be made from high quality wine that has the basic characteristics of vintage port. These wines improve in the bottle.

Tawny This is a blend of ports from a number of harvests aged for a longer period of time in wood. The wines gradually lose

Opposite
Harvest-time in the
Douro Valley. These
are the steep slopes
of the Quinta do
Noval estate. The
baskets of grapes
are taken down the
slopes ready for the
next stage.

their ruby red color and become a mature tawny color, and take on a spicy character. Tawny port is bottled "ready to drink" (the label shows the date of bottling) and is served lightly chilled after dinner. It is bottled after three years in the cask.

Old Tawnies are of a higher standard and of limited quantity. Old tawnies of ten, 15, and 20 years are blends of various top quality ports matured in oak. The year on the label is the average age of the blend.

Colheita is a single-harvest tawny made from high quality wines aged in wood for at least seven years until the wine becomes rich and smooth in character. The label must state the year of harvest, together with the date of bottling.

BOTTLE-AGED ports include crusted, traditional late-bottled vintage, and vintage.

Crusted A blend of high quality wines from a number of years, this port wine is bottled without filtration so that the wine throws a crust (a sediment) as it ages in the bottle. These rich, dark, full-flavored wines should be decanted in the same way as a vintage port.

Late-bottled Vintage is a premium ruby port wine made from a single vintage,

although not necessarily a declared vintage. It is bottled after spending a minimum of five, and a maximum of six, years in wood. The wines have more depth and complexity than a ruby port. Most wines are bottled "ready to drink," but a few, labeled with the word "Traditional," will age further in the bottle.

Single Quinta Vintage This is port from a single harvest and an individual *quinta*.

Above
Baskets of grapes
ready to be taken to
the crusher for the
fermentation stage.

Bottled as a vintage port, the wine matures and throws a crust as it ages in bottle.

Vintage port This is port wine from a single vintage that has been bottled after two to three years in wood. It matures in the bottle until ready to drink. The port may be a blend of wines from several vineyards or made with wines from a single *quinta*. The wine is of a year selected by the shipper as being outstanding. Most vintage ports require between ten and 15 years in the bottle before drinking.

The wine can be sold by the bottle only under the Seal of Guarantee (*Selo de Guarantia*) and should be bottled between July 1 of the second year and June 30 of the third year. A vintage is declared to the trade in the spring of the second year after the harvest, and will be offered to the public that autumn when the wine is bottled.

HOW PORT IS MADE

Port is a fortified wine, made by adding grape spirit or brandy (*aguardente*) to partially fermented red wine (similar in style to a burgundy). This stops fermentation and leaves the wine sweet, rich, and strong in alcohol. Once fortified, the wine stays in the oak cask at the *quinta's* lodges for at least two years before it is bottled.

The vintage takes place in late September or early October and once the grapes of that year have been gathered and made into wine, the "year" begins. Grapes are dumped into a crusher where the juice is released. Juice and the mass of grapes (the "must") is then put into a *lagar* (traditional stone trough) or a stainless steel fermentation tank where the must ferments for two to three days. During this process the natural sugar turns into alcohol.

The juice from the fermentation tank is run off into a *tonel* (large wooden container). Here, the fortification takes place. Grape alcohol is added, which stops the process of fermentation. The remaining must in the fermentation container is pressed two or three times.

Commendable Vintage Port Years

Excellent
1908
1912
1927
1937
1945
1948
1963
1977
1985
1992
1994

Very Good
1931
1938
1942
1955
1958
1960
1966
1970
1975
1983
1991

The young port stays in the casks until the spring following the harvest, when it is taken from the Douro vineyard estate to the city of Vila Nova de Gaia, which faces the city of Oporto located on the opposite bank of the Douro River. It is stored in long, low buildings, called lodges, in casks called pipes (*pipas*), or in larger wooden vats. It stays here for another year and is checked regularly for quality.

Blending begins in February of the second year after the vintage. The final blend is made a few months later, and samples are then submitted to the Instituto do Vinho do Porto for approval. Then the port is bottled without going through either a stabilization or filtration process.

DRINKING AND SERVING PORT

Many of us have been brought up to believe that port wine is solely an after-dinner drink, no doubt due to the amount of attention given to the vintage ports. Yet port wine was once also taken at other times of the day. Early in the 1900s it was fashionable to consume a glass of port with a biscuit or a piece of cake during the hours between 11 a.m. and 1 p.m. The French drink port wine as an aperitif and consume far more port than the British!

All bottles of port should be laid down, not kept upright, while in the cellar. There is no need to decant tawny, or ruby port. You merely pour it at room temperature.

Vintage port needs to be decanted because it is aged in the bottle and a lot of sediment develops. It will become drier, less syrupy, and more mellow in time. When you take a bottle from the cellar or wine rack, where it has probably been lying for some years, stand the bottle upright for 24–48 hours or more to allow it to reach room temperature. This will also help all of the sediment to settle to the bottom of the bottle.

OPENING THE BOTTLE

The cork will be long and sometimes it is difficult to pull, especially when the cork is very old, and may even crumble. Make sure

Opposite

Crushing the freshly picked grapes in the old-fashioned way meant using foot power.

Any time you are not drinking port is a waste of time.

THE LATE PERCY CROFT

you have a long thread on the corkscrew. Place the corkscrew in the center of the cork and slowly push it in, making sure it is in to the full length of the cork. Remove the cork gently.

Here in an effective way to open a bottle with a cork that is too tight to draw or is old and crumbly. Take off the seal, which is made of either wax or lead (or, if it is a newer bottle, plastic). Hold the bottle, wrapped in a slightly damp cloth napkin or towel, firmly at a 45-degree angle. Using the flat edge of a heavy carving knife, hit gently but firmly upward against the flange (lip), turning the bottle slightly after each knock, completing a circle.

If you are successful, the neck will crack cleanly below the flange. Using a cloth to protect your hand from getting cut, take firm hold of the top of the glass neck, complete with the cork, and pull it out.

Now that the bottle is open, take a port or wine funnel (the best ones are curved) and place it in the neck of the decanter. Put a piece of fine muslin cloth over the existing filter in the port funnel. With the label on the bottle facing upward, pour with a steady hand to make sure any crust stays to the bottom of the bottle. It helps to have a lit candle placed next to the decanter

so that the light shines through the dark glass, revealing any bits of sediment that might appear. Leave as much sediment at the bottom of the bottle as possible.

HOW LONG IN THE DECANTER?

A young vintage port will last several days in a decanter. An old port will last just one or two days. The more air in the decanter, the less time it will remain enjoyable to drink.

Opposite
Port is tested and tasted at regular intervals during the production process for texture and color.

Before the 18th century, port wine was sold at public auction in London at Sales by the Candle, when it was customary for parcels to be sold in London coffee houses. Here, the time given for the bidding for a parcel was determined by the time it took for one inch of the auctioneer's candle to burn out, at which time the highest bidder secured the parcel.

Opposite

Posters created in 1910 for an advertising campaign by the House of Ramos-Pinto presented the concept of Bachanalian feasts.

HOW LONG WILL VINTAGE PORT LAST IN THE BOTTLE?

I am often asked this question and I always say that you should never be afraid to open a very old bottle. Because of its 25% alcohol content, it will never become vinegary. In extreme old age (if you have a bottle that's very, very old, you're a lucky person!), the port will have lost its color—it will be more rusty than deep and rich—but it will still be drinkable.

THE GLASS

In most high quality hotel bars and in many homes, port will be served in a regular 2–3oz (6–9cl) port glass. I prefer, when I am at home, to serve port in a small, narrow white wine glass. This shape retains the bouquet which, as you swirl the port around the glass, goes straight to the nose.

Many people prefer a different type of glass for a vintage port from the one they use for a tawny port. There is a reason for this. The bouquet of a vintage port is more generous than that of a tawny port and requires a glass with breathing space.

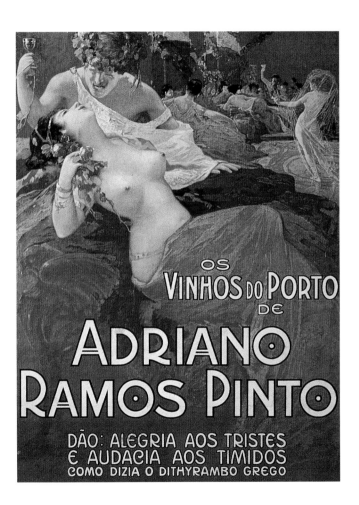

CHAPTER FIVE

LINGERING WITH:
LIQUEURS

■

SWEET AND LUSCIOUS ON THE PALATE, LIQUEURS ARE NOW BACK IN FASHION. ALWAYS SEDUCTIVE, ALWAYS MYSTERIOUS AND EVEN NAUGHTY, THE LIQUEUR IS THE PERFECT END TO A DINNER PARTY.

Opposite
A 1909 poster image for Para liqueur emphasises the femininity of such a drink.

Aaah, liqueurs. The very word conjures up an exquisite small glass, with a stem that looks so fine you might break it. Delicacy and decorum prevail in this after-dinner scenario. Some may even go as far as to say that liqueurs are a feminine drink. Certainly in their original manifestation, liqueurs such as Bénédictine, Chartreuse, and Drambuie were imbibed by both sexes for medicinal purposes.

A liqueur is not a cordial, and I hope this chapter explains the true distilled liqueur clearly. The word "liqueur" comes from the Latin word *liquefacere,* meaning to melt or dissolve. Therefore, a liqueur is the result of the liquefying of its ingredients.

Many of us perhaps first tasted a liqueur at our parents' knees, begging for a sip of the sweet and colorful mixture they poured for themselves and guests after dinner.

Liqueurs are a romantic element of the alcoholic beverages business. Many were originally distilled from a secret recipe kept in the vaults, handed down from one distiller in the family to the next, its secret never revealed. These sweet mysteries of life can trace their origins back to the Middle Ages and the religious monks and apothecaries who created potions and medicines to cure various ailments. Many of these cures were unpleasant to taste so herb and fruit essences were added to mask the bitter flavors.

According to historians, the first documented liqueur was a preparation made from caraway (called kummel) and distilled in 1575 by Lucas Bols in Holland. Bols knew that caraway was good for the digestive system and he hoped it would prove popular when combined with the anesthetic effect of alcohol .

In the rest of Europe, most of the research into the medicinal properties of local herbs and berries was carried out by monks. One of the most famous liqueurs with religious origins is Bénédictine, which can be traced back to the year 1510. Chartreuse was made for the brothers at an abbey in northern France before it became

Opposite
The gentleman at the bar in this German advertisement (dated 1922) confirms that both men and women drank liqueurs during the 1920s and 1930s.

widely available in 1848. It is a favorite *digestif* as well as a great mixer. Today many traditional liqueurs are used in recipes for both pre- and after-dinner cocktails.

MAKING LIQUEURS

Brandy, cognac, whisky, rum, and other spirits are used as the base for many liqueurs. Fruits, plants, seeds, fruit skins, or roots are placed in alcohol in a still, heated, and their vapors are condensed. When cool, this becomes the aromatic spirit.

The other process used is called maceration. It is used only for fruit with pulp—raspberries, blackcurrants, and strong aromatic plants such as tea. When picked, the fruits are put into vats with alcohol and they remain there for weeks. The result is called an infusion.

Note: A crème and a cream are different things. A crème means a liqueur with a flavor. A cream means a combination of alcohol and dairy cream—for example, Bailey's Irish Cream.

THE LIQUEURS
AMARETTO

The Saronno brand produced in the town of the same name is the original trademarked product, yet there are other brands of amaretto. An almond and apricot

Opposite

One of the stylish advertisements from the archives of Amaretto di Saronno shows a sense of fun can be achieved by a sip of this liqueur.

liqueur, it was created by the widow who modeled for the Madonna in the Adoration of the Magi fresco in the Santa Maria delle Grazie sanctuary in Saronno. In appreciation of the honor the widow, who ran the inn at which the painter was staying, created the liqueur for him from plants in her garden. Both the bitter almond and the apricot are from the *Prunus* genus and these combine harmoniously with the 15 other ingredients.

BAILEY'S IRISH CREAM

One of the most popular liqueurs today, this is the original Irish cream liqueur. There are countless imitators trying to emulate the instant success of this smoothie that was introduced to our palates in the 1970s. A mixture of Irish whiskey and dairy cream, it took charge both of our taste buds and a quarter share of the liqueurs market.

BÉNÉDICTINE D.O.M.

(*Deo Optimo Maximo*—'To God, most good, most great")

This drink was made from 27 herbs and spices by Don Bernardo Vincelli, a Benedictine monk at an abbey in France, in 1510. The abbey was destroyed during the French Revolution but, in 1863, one of his descendants regained the recipe, recreated

the elixir, and named it. Bénédictine is made from 27 herbs and spices including nutmeg, hyssop, and thyme.

CHARTREUSE

A French herb liqueur made by Carthusian monks from a secret blend of 130 herbs, plants, honey, and brandy. It is aged for three years. The recipe dates back to 1605. There are several styles: green chartreuse, the original; yellow, which is lighter and sweeter; Chartreuse V.E.P., aged for up to 20 years in oak casks; and Elixir Végétal de la Grande-Chartreuse, which is an herbal liqueur/tonic.

COINTREAU

A French orange liqueur that sells more than a million cases a year. It is a triple sec Curaçao created in the 1850s by Edouard Cointreau after experimentation with both bitter and sweet dried orange peels.

DRAMBUIE

(The name is a phonetic rendering of the Scottish phrase *dram buidheach*—"the drink that satisfies")
Made from a mixture of Scottish herbs and Scotch, its ancestry goes back to the 1740s and Bonnie Prince Charlie. It was not produced commerically until 1906. Honey and herbs are added to a syrup. This is then added to a blend of malt and grain Scotch.

GALLIANO
Created in 1896 by Armando Vaccari as a tribute to the Italian hero Giuseppe Galliano, it is a mixture of 40 herbs and other botanicals, including vanilla and anise.

GRAND MARNIER
A French cognac-spirit based orange liqueur introduced in 1880 by the Lapostolle family after a series of experiments with cognac and bitter oranges from Haiti.

IRISH MIST
The legendary Irish whiskey liqueur made partly with Tullamore whiskey.

KAHLUA
A coffee liqueur made in Mexico from cane spirit, Mexican coffee, and vanilla. It is the world's second biggest-selling liqueur.

KUMMEL
A very popular *digestif*, made from a neutral spirit flavored with caraway seeds, that was originally created in 1575 by the Dutch distiller, Lucas Bols.

LEMONCELLO
An Italian lemon-flavored liqueur from the Amalfi coast that dates back many centuries. It is an infusion made from

Opposite
"The End of an Expensive Evening at Maxim's in Paris."
The frivolity depicted in this 1901 illustration was, of course, caused by the consumption of quite a few after-dinner drinks.

lemonpeel, sugar, and water, combined with a neutral spirit.

MANDARINE NAPOLÉON
Launched in 1892, it is a Belgian tangerine and cognac liqueur. It has seductive overtones—Napoléon was supposed to have given a similar drink to the famous and beautiful Madame Mars in the hope that it would enamor her to his advances.

POLMOS GOLDWASSER
From the Polish vodka producers, a sweet liqueur with minute flakes of gold in spirit, as well as over 12 botanicals, including anise and caraway. Its history can be traced back to the late 1500s.

ROYAL MINT CHOCOLATE
Launched in the 1960s by producer Peter Hallgarten, this French after-dinner drink was composed to taste like the flavor of an after-dinner mint.

SAMBUCA
An aniseed-flavored liqueur made in Italy. (Anise has a fascinating association with medicinal drinks in Italy as far back as the first century AD.)

Usually served with three coffee beans on the surface, which has coined the phrase *con mosca*—with flies.

SOUTHERN COMFORT
This is not a bourbon! A peach-flavored American liqueur with a spirit base and more than 100 ingredients, it was created in the 1890s by a New Orleans bartender trying to improve the basic whiskey he had to serve.

STREGA (ITALIAN FOR "WITCH")
In 1860 the Alberti family in Benevento, southern Italy, created this herbal liqueur. It is made from over 70 botanicals macerated in grain spirit, redistilled in pot stills,and then aged in oak and ash vats before a coloring—saffron—is added. The aroma features a hint of mint with fennel leaf.

TIA MARIA
A Jamaican coffee liqueur with a chocolate finish that was first made in the 1600s.

MAJOR BRANDS
Bols, De Kuyper, and Marie Brizard are just three of the major companies that make a wide range of genuine liqueurs, including apricot, cherry, and blackberry flavors, curaçao, crème de cacao, crème de fraises, crème de menthe, crème de prunelle, and crème de vanille. Each year companies such as these look for unique flavors. There is even a liqueur that has the exotic flavor of orchids.

SERVING LIQUEURS

Opposite

The Dutch liqueur house Bols used stylised artwork to great effect in their early advertising campaigns.

Always serve a liqueur at room temperature and in a small, specially designed liqueur glass. A liqueur is to be sipped, not gulped (you can always have a second glass!) since each has a specific flavor and aroma of its own that are best savored slowly.

Preferably drink a liqueur after coffee. The current fashion for serving liqueurs—Cointreau, Bailey's Irish Cream, kummel, and Drambuie—on ice in an old-fashioned glass does no real harm to the flavor but it does dilute the strength. However, how you drink your liqueur is a personal choice.

BOLS

BITTERS &
MEDICINAL DIGESTIFS

These include ancient types of herbal bitters made by the apothecaries. They are called "bitters" because they are made from herbs, roots, and other botanicals and contain less sugar and less fruit pulp than regular liqueurs.

ANGOSTURA

Angostura is the result of study by a Prussian army surgeon, Dr. J. G. B. Siegert, during a posting to Bolivia. The stomach-settler is named after the city of Angostura and has a rum base mixed with gentian root and many other "secret" herbs.

FERNET-BRANCA

This herbal digestif dates back to the early 1800s but was commercialized in 1845 by the Italian Fratelli Branca distillery. Gentian, rhubarb, and saffron are among the 30 herbs in the original recipe, which is adhered to today by the producers.

JAGERMEISTER

A German product introduced in 1935 which includes 56 botanicals among which are anise, poppy seeds, and ginseng.

RAMAZZOTTI

An Italian brand that dates back to 1815,

when Ausano Ramazzotti mixed 33 herbs and roots, including gentian, orange peel, angelica, and anise, with alcohol spirit. He opened a café near La Scala Opera House and served this *amaro* (Italian for "bitters") instead of the usual coffee.

UNDERBERG

Hubert Underberg founded his company in 1846 to produce a natural herbal *digestif* from herbs from 43 countries. The company is still family-run, and the product is still marketed in a small bottle containing just enough mixture to settle the stomach after a rich meal.

THE RECIPES

■

M IXING AFTER-DINNER DRINKS IS A FUN
RITUAL AND A CONVERSATION POINT FOR
GUESTS. ALL YOU NEED ARE THE BEST
INGREDIENTS AND AN ELEGANT GLASS.

It is important to drink from a glass that looks as delicious as the after-dinner cocktail it contains—when the glass touches the lip it shouldn't intrude between the sip and the lip.

Use your imagination when choosing your set of glasses. These days glasses are designer items, with colorful stems and intriguing shapes with cut glass that reflects a myriad of images. Taking all of these aspects into consideration, remember that simplicity of line and style is the best.

All measurements are given in fluid ounces (oz) (imperial) first, followed by centiliters (cl) (metric). The measurements given are for one drink only.

The recipe will advise you when to chill a glass. Most of the drinks are ungarnished.

NOTE: Some original recipes ask for the *digestif* liqueur curaçao, which was popular in the 1920s and 30s. The original curaçao was made from grape spirit, sugar, and

Opposite
An advertising posters conceived in the 1920s style by the artist Réne Vincent for the port producers, Ramos-Pinto.

orange peel. These days many curaçaos are produced in varying flavors and colors. The recipe, however, should use only the orange flavored liqueur. If you cannot find curaçao, use Triple Sec or Cointreau.

EQUIPMENT

Making a superb after-dinner drink is simple. Add the ingredients in the correct proportions and stir or shake them with the right ice (ice that doesn't crumble when you shake it, and ice that is not too "wet"). Use the best glass for the specific drink and you will have perfection.

THE MIXING GLASS

This technique is used when you want to cool the ingredients without "bruising" them. The point is to avoid breaking the ice and therefore diluting the drink. This method is ideal for drinks that do not contain juices or dairy products. Many classics are made this way, for instance, Alaska and Chicago.

1. Half-fill the mixing glass with pure, dry ice and stir the ice with a barspoon three to four times to chill the mixing glass.
2. Using the bar strainer, remove the excess water created by this process.
3. Add the ingredients and stir briefly and

energetically in a circular motion with the barspoon for about ten seconds.

4. Insert the strainer and pour into the appropriate chilled glasses.

THE COCKTAIL SHAKER

There are three main types of shaker:

a) The Continental, which consists of two pieces of metal;

b) The Boston, which consists of one metal and one glass piece;

c) The Classic, which consists of three metal pieces and incorporates a funnel.

Before using the shaker, make sure it is clean and free of any odor from previous use.

1. Quarter-fill with ice and shake. Strain the excess water as with the mixing glass.

2. Add the ingredients, using the cheapest first to minimize any mistakes.

3. Do not overfill the shaker.

4. Do not use carbonated ingredients.

5. Make sure the shaker is sealed before you shake it.

6. When pouring more than one drink, fill the glasses to equal level on the first passing, and gradually add more to each glass to make them even. If each glass is not full enough, make a bit more mixture to fill up the glasses. This gives a consistency in the mixture.

7. If the lid of the shaker becomes stuck, it can be eased by warming the point where it joins the body of the shaker. This happens because you have shaken the mixture for too long and the shaker becomes frozen. Rub it with a cloth and it will loosen.

Hint: Do not shake the ingredients to death! Shake sharply for six to ten seconds.

TO LAYER

This is a traditional, popular technique used since pre-Prohibition days. All it requires is a steady hand. Spirits, liqueurs, syrups, cream, and juices vary in density and weight. You can create attractive and colorful drinks by pouring each ingredient carefully over a barspoon. Always start with the heaviest liquid. Each ingredient will lay one on top of the other. I prefer to use the "bowl" of the barspoon to allow the liquid to float off the barspoon onto the previous layer in the glass.

GLASS TYPES AND SIZES

Cocktail:	4oz (11cl)
Old-fashioned:	10oz (30cl)
Shot:	2–3oz (6–9cl)
Brandy balloon:	12oz (35cl)
Liqueur:	2–3oz (6–9cl)
Port:	2–3oz (6–9cl)

AFTER-DINNER SPECIAL

This was a popular drink in the late 1920s in both the U.S. and Europe. It has a smooth, delicate texture, and the orange and apricot flavors combine very well.

Pour the ingredients into a shaker with ice. Shake. Strain into a chilled cocktail glass.

METHOD: shake

1⅓oz/4cl apricot brandy
1oz /3cl curaçao

AFTER-EIGHT

This drink has a delicious creamy mint flavor.

Pour the whisky, chocolate liqueur, and cream in a shaker with ice. Shake and strain into a chilled cocktail glass. Garnish with a sprig of fresh mint and grate a fine layer of chocolate on top of the mixture. If you cannot find Royal Mint chocolate liqueur, add a drop of white crème de menthe into a chocolate liqueur to achieve the same flavor. Serve.

METHOD: shake

⅔oz/2cl Scotch whisky
⅔oz/2cl mint chocolate liqueur (Royal Mint)
1⅓oz/4cl fresh cream

ALASKA

Writing in *The Savoy Cocktail Book*, Harry Craddock comments: "So far as can be ascertained, this delectable potion is NOT the staple diet of the Esquimaux (sic.). It was probably first thought of in South Carolina—hence its name."

Stir the gin and Chartreuse in a mixing glass until completely mixed. Strain into a chilled cocktail glass. (Some recipes recommend shaking this drink but this gives a cloudy effect to the drink. I prefer it mixed.)

METHOD: stir

1¾oz/5cl gin
⅔oz/2cl yellow
  Chartreuse

Opposite
Alaska.

ALEXANDER NO. 1

A classic 1920s after-dinner drink that will spice up the evening.

Pour the ingredients into a shaker with ice. Strain into a chilled cocktail glass. Shake. Sprinkle a fine layer of nutmeg on top of the drink—just enough to get the aroma of the nutmeg. It shouldn't overpower the flavor of the drink.

METHOD: shake

1oz/3cl gin
1oz/3cl white crème de
  cacao
1oz/3cl fresh cream

ALEXANDER No. 2

METHOD: shake

1oz/3cl brandy
1oz/3cl white crème de cacao
1oz/3cl fresh cream

This is the 1920s pale relation to the popular classic Brandy Alexander, which uses brown crème de cacao.

Pour ingredients into a shaker with ice. Shake. Strain into a chilled cocktail glass.

ALEXANDER SISTERS

METHOD: shake

1oz/3cl gin
1oz/3cl green crème de menthe
1oz/3cl fresh cream

Yet another Alexander relation, this drink was considered risqué in the late 1920s, and could possibly lead a young woman astray.

Pour ingredients into a shaker with ice. Shake and strain into a chilled cocktail glass. Garnish with a sprig of mint on the side of the glass.

AMBER CLOUD

METHOD: shake

1⅓oz/4cl cognac
⅔oz/2cl Galliano

Sip this to get the aroma of the cognac and the fragrance of the Galliano.

Pour the ingredients in a shaker with ice. Shake to create a cloud, then pour into an old-fashioned glass filled with crushed ice and serve with a short straw.

Opposite
Amber Cloud.

ANGEL'S DELIGHT

A classic layered drink that delivers individual flavors with each sip.

Pour the grenadine into a shot glass then, over a barspoon, gently add the Triple Sec and crème de Yvette and, finally, the cream. The result is a drink of colorful layers because each of the ingredients has a different density.

METHOD: layer

½oz/1.5cl grenadine
½oz/1.5cl Triple Sec (or Cointreau)
½oz/1.5cl crème de Yvette (or parfait amour)
½oz/1.5cl fresh cream

ANGEL'S DREAM

Perfect for a late fall evening when you've spent most of the day getting by on a wing and prayer.

Pour the maraschino into a shot or liqueur glass then, using a barspoon, carefully add the crème de Yvette and, lastly, the cognac.

METHOD: layer

1oz/3cl maraschino
1oz/3cl crème de Yvette (or parfait amour)
1oz/3cl cognac

Opposite
*Left: Angel's Delight;
right, Angel's Dream.*

ANGEL FACE

METHOD: shake

1oz/3cl gin
1oz/3cl apricot brandy
1oz/3cl calvados

In the 1950s you could find two or three recipes with this name that used different ingredients and were made in different ways. One used crème de cacao and fresh cream, the other was similar to a pousse café (layered) formula, made with crème de cacao and prunelle (sloe) brandy. This recipe is the classic, creating a soft, perfumed drink; indulgent, with a round and uplifting finish.

Pour all ingredients into a shaker with ice. Shake. Strain into a chilled cocktail glass.

ANGEL'S KISS

METHOD: layer

½oz/1.5cl white
  crème de cacao
½oz/1.5cl prunelle (sloe)
  brandy
½oz/1.5cl crème de
  Yvette (or parfait
  amour)
½oz/1.5cl fresh cream

A smooth, creamy drink with a heightened sense of chocolate and a hint of prune. Sweet all the way, like the kiss of an angel.

In a liqueur glass, pour first the white crème de cacao then, using a barspoon, pour the prunelle (sloe) brandy, the crème de Yvette, and the fresh cream.

ANGEL'S TIP

A quick and easy after-dinner drink that leaves you with a sweet and smooth aftertaste.

Pour the brown crème de cacao into a liqueur glass and float the cream on top. Garnish with a red cherry on a toothpick.

METHOD: layer

1oz/3cl brown crème de cacao
1oz/3cl fresh cream

ANGEL'S WING

A 1930s classic with the ability to take you higher.

Pour the white crème de cacao over a barspoon, into a liqueur glass, followed by the prunelle (sloe) brandy. The finishing touch is a dash of fresh cream.

METHOD: layer

1oz/3cl white crème de cacao
1oz/3cl prunelle (sloe) brandy
Dash of fresh cream

APOTHECARY COCKTAIL

METHOD: stir

1oz/3cl Fernet Branca
1oz/3cl white crème de
menthe
1oz/3cl Carpano
(Punt e mes)

This is a wonderful *digestif* to serve at the end of a heavy dinner. The combination of the Fernet Branca and the white crème de menthe, with the mellowness of the Carpano, settles the digestive system.

Pour all the ingredients in a mixing glass filled with ice and stir. Strain into a chilled cocktail glass and serve.

B & B

METHOD: build

1oz/3cl brandy
1oz/3cl Bénédictine

A popular old classic drink that is sold premixed in many stores. Another version of this drink, called A & B, uses armagnac and Bénédictine.

Pour the brandy directly into a brandy balloon and gently add the Bénédictine.

B P

METHOD: build

1oz/3cl brandy
⅔oz/2cl ruby port

This is an excellent, much-appreciated *digestif* and a good medicine for a stomach upset.

Pour the port into a port glass, followed by the brandy. Stir. Serve.

B - 5 2

This is by far one of the most popular "shooter" drinks—a leftover from the indulgent mid-1980's. One brilliant way to drink this mix is to light the top of the drink with a match, put a regular straw into the bottom of the glass, and suck the liquid up quickly in one long but quick movement.

Pour the Kahlua into a liqueur glass first, then add the Bailey's over a barspoon, and finally the Grand Marnier, also over a barspoon. The result is an orange flavor, with a hint of creamy whisky, and a coffee finish.

METHOD: layer

⅔oz/2cl Kahlua
⅔oz/2cl Bailey's Irish Cream
⅔oz/2cl Grand Marnier

BANANA BLISS

A creamy creation from the Southern Hemisphere that encapsulates all that is exotic.

Pour the cognac into a mixing glass, followed by the banana liqueur. Stir, then strain into an old-fashioned glass. This combination produces a wonderful golden liquid with the strength of the cognac and the unique overlay of banana.

METHOD: stir

1⅓oz/4cl cognac
1oz/3cl banana liqueur

BARBARA

METHOD: shake

1oz/3cl vodka
1oz/3cl white crème de
   cacao
1oz/3cl fresh cream

A 1930s classic that brings back memories of an elegant era.

Pour all ingredients in a shaker with ice. Strain and pour into a chilled cocktail glass. The result is a pale, creamy drink with a touch of froth. Garnish with a sprinkle of fresh grated nutmeg.

BETWEEN THE SHEETS

METHOD: shake

1oz/3cl white rum
1oz/3cl Cointreau
1oz/3cl brandy
Dash of lemon juice

Perfect for a late-night encounter dedicated to seduction. Obviously successful since the drink has been around since the 1920s. This has the spiciness of the rum, the velvety, orange flavor of the Cointreau, and the strength of the brandy (you'll need it later). The lemon adds a sharpness to keep you alert. Rich and intense like the possibilities it offers . . .

Pour all ingredients into a shaker with ice and shake. Strain into a chilled cocktail glass.

Opposite
Left; Barbara;
right, Blackjack.

— Deres Frues Skaal, Hr. Kaptejn!
— Tak, Frue! — Deres Smaa's!

BELMONT COCKTAIL

In the 1920s the combination of gin and grenadine was seen as daring, like a flash of red lipstick.

Pour all ingredients into a shaker with ice. Shake. Strain into a chilled cocktail glass.

METHOD: shake

1/⅓oz/4cl gin
½oz /1½cl grenadine
1oz/3cl fresh cream

BLACKJACK

For anyone who likes to while away the hours at the casino table . . . drink before you play, not during!

Pour all ingredients into a shaker with ice. Shake. Strain into an old-fashioned glass filled with ice.

METHOD: shake

1oz/3cl kirsch
1oz/3cl iced coffee
½oz 1½cl brandy

BLACK RUSSIAN

At the height of its popularity in the 1950s, this vodka drink with a dark finish is enjoying a resurgence.

Pour the vodka directly into an old-fashioned glass with ice and add the Kahlua. Stir.

METHOD: build

1⅓oz/4cl vodka
⅔oz/2cl Kahlua

Opposite
An illustration from a Danish magazine dated 1903 depicting an after-dinner toast.

Blanche Cocktail

METHOD: shake

1oz/3cl anisette
1oz/3cl Cointreau
1oz/3cl white curaçao

A classic dating from the 1920s creating a pale and interesting vision.

Pour all ingredients in a shaker with ice. Shake. Strain into a chilled cocktail glass.

Block and Fall

METHOD: shake

⅔oz/2cl brandy
⅔oz/2cl Cointreau
½oz/1½cl Pernod
½oz/1½cl calvados

This drink was created by a T. van Dycke at the Ciro Club, Deauville, France, in 1924. It was originally made with absinthe instead of Pernod, creating an aphrodisiac drink. Too many of these and someone will have to block your fall . . . unless you're headed for a soft landing.

Pour all ingredients into a shaker with ice. Shake. Strain into a chilled cocktail glass.

Blushin' Russian

METHOD: shake

1oz/3cl vodka
½oz/1½cl Kahlua
½oz/1½cl amaretto
½oz/1½cl fresh cream

A passionate drink with a hint of three volatile nations—Russia, Mexico, and Italy—tempered by the cream.

Pour all ingredients into a shaker with ice. Shake. Strain into a chilled cocktail glass.

BOSOM CARESSER

A 1920s classic first made by Harry Craddock at the American Bar at London's Savoy Hotel. Sweet Madeira can be added to this recipe to give a smoother taste.

Pour all ingredients into a shaker with ice. Shake. Strain into a chilled cocktail glass.

METHOD: shake

1⅓oz/4cl brandy
⅔oz/2cl curaçao
Dash of grenadine
1 egg yolk

BOTTOMS UP

One from the late 1940s. A rich and powerful drink to sip, and when you see the bottom of the glass, it's time to retire to bed.

Van der Hum, a delicious tangerine-and-orange-flavored liqueur, is from South Africa. It gives this drink a unique color and flavor.

Pour all ingredients into a shaker with ice. Shake. Strain into a chilled cocktail glass.

METHOD: shake

1oz/3cl cognac
⅔oz/2cl Van der Hum
½oz/1½cl fresh cream
1 egg yolk
Dash of grenadine

BRANDY ALEXANDER

By far one of the most sophisticated after-dinner drinks, this was at the height of its popularity in the heady 1960s and 70s and is still popular. When I visited The Mansion, Turtle Creek in Dallas, I noticed they used the same spirit ingredients but replaced the cream with a scoop of vanilla ice cream, and used a blender. An interesting variation.

Pour all ingredients into a shaker with ice. Shake. Strain into a chilled cocktail glass. Garnish with a sprinkle of freshly grated nutmeg.

METHOD: shake

1oz/3cl brandy
1oz/3cl brown crème de cacao
1oz/3cl fresh cream

BRANDY COCKTAIL

A 1920s classic drink with a bitter sweet finish—like the end of a wonderful romance with someone you still yearn for.

*Pour the ingredients into a mixing glass with ice. Stir. Strain into a balloon glass. *The original recipe did not use Angostura bitters. This was added to the mixture at a later stage and gives it that something extra!*

METHOD: mixing glass

1¾oz /5cl brandy
2 dashes curaçao
2 dashes Angostura bitters

Opposite
Brandy Alexander.

123

B R A V E   B U L L

A classic drink with a kick from the tequila disguised by the softness of the Kahlua. Not for the fainthearted.

Pour the tequila and the Kahlua into an old-fashioned glass filled with ice.

METHOD: build

1⅓oz /4cl tequila
⅔oz/2cl Kahlua

C H A R L E S '   N I G H T C A P

This combination gives an interesting, powerful, and fruity flavor.

Pour the ingredients into a mixing glass with ice and stir. Strain into a brandy balloon glass.

METHOD: stir

1⅓oz/4cl armagnac
1oz/3cl pear schnapps

Opposite
*Left: Sweet Sue;
right, Chicago.*

C H I C A G O   C O C K T A I L

A 1920–1930 classic after-dinner drink with its origins in the Speakeasy culture.

Rub a slice of lemon around the rim of a chilled cocktail glass, dip into powdered sugar, and add ice. Add the first three ingredients to a mixing glass, stir, and strain into the cocktail glass. Add champagne to give it that spark of life.

METHOD: stir

2oz/6cl brandy
Dash of Angostura
   bitters
Dash of curaçao (Triple
   Sec or Cointreau)
1oz/3cl champagne

COFFEE GRASSHOPPER

METHOD: shake

1oz/3cl Kahlua
1oz/3cl white crème de menthe
1oz/3cl fresh cream

A coffee-and-mint-flavored drink with the cream adding a smoothness.

Pour the ingredients into a shaker with ice. Shake. Strain into a chilled cocktail glass.

COGNAC MINT FRAPPÉ

METHOD: build

1oz/3cl cognac
1oz/3cl green crème de menthe
3–4 fresh mint leaves
½ teaspoon of sugar

The fragrance of the cognac and the crème de menthe combines well with the fresh aroma of the crushed mint leaves. The sugar brings out the full mint flavor in an instant. A really great *digestif*.

Place the mint leaves in an old-fashioned glass and add ½ teaspoon of sugar. Crush the leaves and sugar together with the back of a barspoon (or a wooden muddler) to bring out the essence of the mint. Add the spirits and stir. Fill the glass with crushed ice and stir again. Serve with a straw.

You can use any liqueur and more than one ingredient to make a frappé—the word frappé means a drink that is served with finely crushed ice.

Opposite
Crème de Menthe Frappé

COLORADO

METHOD: shake

1oz/3cl kirsch
1oz/3cl cherry brandy
1oz/3cl fresh cream

Strength, vitality, and sweetness are just three of the words to describe this drink's qualities.

Pour all ingredients into a shaker filled with ice. Shake. Strain into a cocktail glass. Garnish with a red maraschino cherry and serve.

COWBOY COCKTAIL

METHOD: shake

2oz/6cl bourbon
1oz/3cl fresh cream

A drink that's been moseying along the trail for over 70 years now and gets better every day.

Pour the bourbon and fresh cream into a shaker with ice. Shake. Strain into an old-fashioned glass filled with crushed ice. Serve with a straw.

CRÈME DE MENTHE FRAPPÉ

METHOD: build

2oz/6cl green crème de menthe
Crushed ice

This is simply a good *digestif* since it gives you a superb, refreshing feeling.

Pour the crème de menthe into an old-fashioned glass filled with finely crushed ice. Serve with a straw.

DIANA COCKTAIL

A 1920s classic immortalized in Harry Craddock's *The Savoy Cocktail Book* for a Diana from another era. This is a fine *digestif*.

Fill an old-fashioned glass with finely crushed ice and pour in the crème de menthe. Gently float the brandy on top. Serve with a short straw.

METHOD: build

1/¾oz/5cl white crème de menthe
⅔oz/2cl brandy

DIRTY MOTHER

A rich, coffee flavor with a strong finish. It is a wonderful, muddy golden color. The name is bemusing (I wish I knew its origin) but, believe me, it's a pleasant drink.

Pour the brandy into an old-fashioned glass with ice and add the Kahlua. Stir.

METHOD: build

1⅓oz/4cl brandy
1oz/3cl Kahlua

DIZZY

I'm so dizzy, my head is spinning … as the old song says, more than one of these will set your head a-spinning. The grappa brings a powerful, grapey, and earthy finish to the woodiness of the bourbon. The addition of the honey brings the touch of sweetness. This is an excellent *digestif.*

Pour the bourbon, grappa, and honey into a shaker with ice. Shake. Strain into a chilled cocktail glass.

METHOD: shake

1⅓oz/4cl bourbon
1oz/3cl grappa
½ teaspoon of liquid
   honey

DOBBS

This is the butler's recommendation for an excellent digestive drink, especially good after a heavy meal late in the evening.

Fill an old-fashioned glass with crushed ice and pour in the crème de menthe. Gently float the Fernet Branca on top. Serve with a straw.

METHOD: build

1¾oz/5cl white crème
   de menthe
⅔oz/2cl Fernet Branca

Opposite
Left: Hot Shot; right,
Dizzy.

DREAM COCKTAIL

METHOD: shake

1¾oz/5cl brandy
1oz/3cl Triple Sec or
 Cointreau
Dash of anisette

A 1920s classic full of promise. It's brandy with an orange flavor and a hint of licorice. These marry well together.

Pour the ingredients into a shaker with ice. Shake. Strain into a chilled cocktail glass.

FERRARI

METHOD: build

1oz/3cl amaretto
1¾oz/5cl dry
 vermouth

Named after my favorite racing car. Speedsters like me will get a buzz from the flavors in this drink.

Pour the amaretto into an old-fashioned glass with ice, then add the vermouth. Stir.

FIFTH AVENUE

METHOD: layer

1oz/3cl apricot brandy
1oz/3cl brown crème
 de cacao
1oz/3cl fresh cream

A 1930s favorite with those who enjoy the taste of apricot combined with the smoothness of creamy chocolate. A great drink to imbibe after going window-shopping down the Avenue.

Carefully pour the brown crème de cacao into a liqueur or shot glass. Then float the apricot brandy over a barspoon on top of the crème de cacao. Finally, float the cream. The result is a delicious, multi-colored drink.

FIRST NIGHT

To make sure this is not the only night ... try a little of this divine drink.

Pour all ingredients into a shaker with ice. Shake. Strain into a chilled cocktail glass.

METHOD: shake

1⅓oz/4cl brandy
½oz /1½cl Van der Hum
½oz/1½cl fresh cream

FORBIDDEN COCKTAIL

The brandy brings a strength to the smoothness of the vanilla-and-chocolate-flavored mixture. It's divine and we've all done something forbidden, so sit back and sip.

Pour all ingredients into a shaker with ice. Shake. Strain into a chilled cocktail glass and garnish with a chocolate stick.

METHOD: shake

1oz/3cl cognac
1oz/3cl crème de vanille
1oz/3cl white crème de cacao

FRENCH CONNECTION

A classic after-dinner drink combining an almond flavor with the richness of brandy. One sip and you are back with actor Gene Hackman under that dangerous New York bridge.

Fill an old-fashioned glass with ice, pour in the brandy and amaretto. Stir and serve.

METHOD: build

1¾oz/3cl brandy
1oz/3cl amaretto

FRENCH KISS

This is a sublime after-dinner drink that has all the trademarks of a raspberry lipstick flavor . . . kiss after kiss after luscious kiss.

Pour the cream, then the vodka, Chambord, and crème de cacao into a shaker with ice. Shake. Strain into a chilled cocktail glass. Garnish with a fresh raspberry in the center of the drink.

METHOD: shake

1oz/3cl vodka
1oz/3cl Chambord liqueur
½oz/1½cl white crème de cacao
½oz/1½cl fresh cream

Opposite
*Left: French Kiss;
right, Grasshopper.*

GODFATHER

A drink that's as deep and mysterious as Marlon Brando's voice in the movie of the same name. It has an almond/apricot base and blends well with the whisky.

Pour both of the ingredients into an old-fashioned glass with ice and stir.

METHOD: build

1¾oz/5cl Scotch (whisky)
1oz/3cl amaretto

GODMOTHER

Same as above.

1¾oz/5cl vodka
1oz/3cl amaretto

GODCHILD

Pour all ingredients into a shaker with ice. Shake. Strain into a chilled cocktail glass.

METHOD: shake

1oz/3cl vodka
1oz/3cl amaretto
1oz/3cl fresh cream

GOLDEN CADILLAC

METHOD: shake

1oz/3cl Galliano
1oz/3cl white crème de cacao
1oz/3cl fresh cream

One of the most popular drinks. One of these and you may be tempted to say *"Baby, you can drive my car . . ."*

Pour the ingredients into a shaker with ice and shake. Strain into a cocktail glass and serve.

GOLDEN DREAM

METHOD: shake

1oz/3cl Galliano
½oz/1½cl Cointreau
½oz/1½cl orange juice
½oz/1½cl fresh cream

A classic with a superb orange flavor and a hint of vanilla from the Galliano. It looks impressive in the glass and tastes like a dream.

Pour the Galliano, Cointreau, and orange juice into a shaker, and then add the cream. Shake. Strain into a chilled cocktail glass and serve.

Opposite
Left; Golden Cadillac;
right, Golden Dream.

GOLDEN SLIPPER

METHOD: shake

1oz/3cl yellow
  Chartreuse
1oz/3cl apricot brandy
1 egg yolk

The original 1920s after-dinner drink contained Eau-de-vie de Danzig but I prefer the taste of these liqueurs. This is also how the drink is served today.

Pour the Chartreuse and the apricot brandy into a shaker with ice first, then add the egg yolk. Shake. Strain into a chilled cocktail glass and serve.

GOLDEN TORPEDO

METHOD: shake

1oz/3cl Galliano
1oz/3cl amaretto
1oz/3cl fresh cream

This is the perfect drink for weakening the defenses.

Pour all ingredients into a shaker with ice. Shake. Strain into a chilled cocktail glass and serve.

GRASSHOPPER

METHOD: shake

1oz/3cl green crème de
  menthe
1oz/3cl white crème de
  cacao
1oz/3cl fresh cream

A classic drink that, along with Brandy Alexander, is one of the top ten after-dinner drinks.

Pour the ingredients into a shaker with ice. Shake. Strain into a chilled cocktail glass and serve.

GREEN DRAGON

A fiery 1920s classic concoction made with one of the most popular liqueurs, kummel. A good *digestif* that can chase away any lingering demons.

Pour the fresh juice followed by the gin, kummel, and crème de menthe into a shaker with ice. Shake. Strain into a chilled cocktail glass and serve.

METHOD: shake

1oz/3cl gin
⅔oz/2cl kummel
⅔oz/2cl green crème de menthe
2 dashes fresh lemon juice
4 dashes peach bitters

HAPPY WORLD

With the combination of flavors and smooth texture, this is guaranteed to make your world seem a little happier, sip after sip after sip.

Pour the brandy and Cointreau, then the juice and banana liqueur, into a shaker with ice. Shake. Strain into a brandy balloon glass.

METHOD: shake

½oz/1½cl brandy
1oz/3cl Cointreau
1oz/3cl orange juice
½oz/1½cl banana liqueur

HOT KISS

METHOD: stir

1oz/3cl Irish whiskey
½oz/1½cl white crème de menthe
½oz/1½cl white crème de cacao
4oz/12cl hot coffee
⅔oz/2cl fresh cream

What more can I say about this drink?

Pour the liqueurs and whiskey into a heat-proof goblet. Add the coffee and stir. Top with the fresh cream and garnish with a dusting of chocolate powder. Serve hot.

HOT SHOT

METHOD: layer

½oz/1½cl cold coffee
½oz/1½cl Galliano
½oz/1½cl fresh cream

A popular drink in Australia, where bartenders compete to see who can make this drink in the fastest time.

Pour the Galliano into a liqueur or shot glass, then rest a barspoon above it and pour the coffee over. Add the cream. Serve and drink in one swallow.

HUNTER

METHOD: build

2oz/6cl bourbon
1oz/3cl cherry brandy

This drink has a smoky aroma and a cherry flavor. A mellow drink for the end of an evening.

Pour the bourbon directly into an old-fashioned glass with ice. Add the cherry brandy and stir. Serve.

Opposite
Left: Hunter; right, Angel's Wing.

IRISH COFFEE

METHOD: build

2 teaspoons brown
  sugar
1¾oz/5cl Irish whiskey
3½oz/10cl hot coffee
⅔oz/2cl double cream

A soothing drink that was born at a freezing cold airfield at Shannon Airport, near Ireland's Atlantic Coast, just after World War Two, it has remained extremely popular. The airport was a refueling stop for transatlantic aircraft and while on the ground, the passengers were refueled by Irishman Joe Sheridan. He took the traditional Irish drink, whiskey in tea, and substituted coffee for tea to suit the Americans' taste. Adding a thick whirl of lightly whipped Irish cream on top, and sugar, he served this in a stemmed glass to his customers.

The first Irish coffee was taken to San Francisco by the late writer Stanton Delaplane and served in 1952 at the Buena Vista bar at Fisherman's Wharf. Now, more than 2,000 Irish coffees are served there each day. Some people serve this in a china mug. I prefer to feel the warmth of glass next to my lips.

Pour the whiskey into a heat-proof, large glass goblet, add the brown sugar and stir. Add the hot coffee and stir with a teaspoon. Gently float the whipped cream by pouring it over a barspoon. Do not stir. Serve while it is hot.

OTHER VERSIONS

This drink has become international—bartenders in Jamaica make Calypso Coffee by adding Tia Maria to hot coffee and cream. In other Caribbean islands, they add rum. Mexicans add Kahlua, Italians add Strega; the French add cognac; Scandinavians add Aquavit; and the British add Drambuie to make Prince Charles Coffee.

Add your favorite liqueur or spirit to make the drink of your choice.

IRISH NUT

Here is a richly smooth after-dinner drink with a nutty flavor.

Pour all ingredients into a shaker with ice. Shake. Strain into a chilled cocktail glass and serve.

METHOD: shake

1oz/3cl Irish whiskey
1oz/3cl Bailey's Irish Cream
1oz/3cl frangelica

ITALIAN SOMBRERO

A relaxing drink for the end of the day.

Pour ingredients into an old-fashioned glass filled with ice and stir.

METHOD: build

2oz/6cl amaretto
1oz/3cl fresh cream

ITALIAN STALLION

METHOD: shake

1oz/3cl amaretto
½oz/1½cl white crème de cacao
½oz/1½cl white crème de noyaux
1oz/3cl fresh cream

Crème de noyaux is a French liqueur made from extracted oils of peach and apricot kernels. It has a delicious flavor that combines well with the other ingredients. A drink created to keep up the reputation of the Italian lover, it's been a favorite in my family for years.

Pour all ingredients into a shaker with ice. Shake. Strain into a chilled cocktail glass and serve.

KENTUCKY COLONEL COCKTAIL

METHOD: stir

2oz/6cl bourbon
1oz/3cl Bénédictine

If there's any finger lickin' to be done, do it after you've served the drink.

Pour the bourbon and the Bénédictine into a mixing glass with ice. Stir, then strain into old-fashioned glass with fresh ice. Serve with a stirrer.

KING CREOLE

As dark as the soul music that gave birth to the blues, here's a rock 'n' roll flavor to savor after dinner.

Pour all ingredients except the cream into a shaker. Shake to the rhythmn. Strain into a chilled cocktail glass and gently float the cream over the top. Serve.

METHOD: shake

1oz/3cl dark rum
½oz/1½cl crème de banana
½oz/1½cl Kahlua
1oz/3cl fresh cream

LADY LOVE COCKTAIL

A wonderful combination: a hint of mint and blackberry with an overlay of orange held together by the ruby port.

Pour all ingredients into a shaker with ice. Shake. Strain into a chilled cocktail glass and serve tenderly.

METHOD: shake

1oz/3cl curaçao
1oz/3cl ruby port
½oz/1½cl white crème de menthe
½oz/1½cl crème de mur (blackberries)

LAST DRINK COCKTAIL

This is the one to have before—before anything wonderful!

Pour all ingredients into a shaker with ice and shake. Strain into a chilled cocktail glass and serve.

METHOD: shake

1oz/3cl cognac
½oz/1½cl yellow Chartreuse
½oz/1½cl cherry brandy
½oz/1½cl kummel

LONDON FOG

METHOD: shake

1oz/3cl white crème de
menthe
1oz/3cl anisette
Few dashes of
Angostura bitters

Not quite the color of a modern London fog but definitely as misty and mysterious. The result of mixing these liquids is a swirling cloudy look caused by the anisette. It is a great *digestif*, with an aniseed flavor.

Pour all ingredients into a shaker with ice and shake. Strain into a chilled cocktail glass. Serve immediately for the best misty effect.

LOUISVILLE LADY

METHOD: shake

1oz/3cl bourbon
½oz/1½cl white crème
de cacao
½oz/1½cl fresh cream

This combination offers a touch of Southern elegance in a rich-tasting after-dinner drink.

Pour the bourbon and the crème de cacao into a shaker with ice. Shake. Strain into a liqueur glass and gently float the fresh cream on top. Serve.

Opposite
*Left: Rattlesnake; right,
London Fog.*

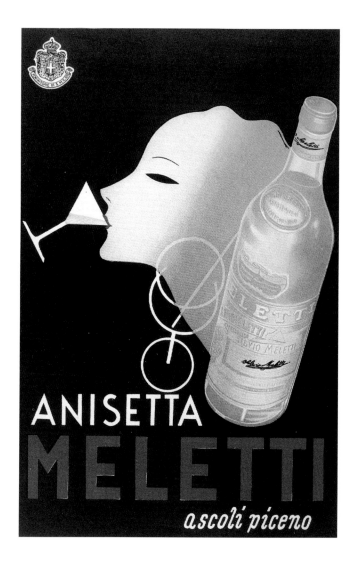

LOVER'S DELIGHT

A fine mixture of cognac and Cointreau is guaranteed to bring tender emotions to the surface. Drink with someone you care for. Do not waste the taste of rich berries and orange on anyone else.

Pour all ingredients into a shaker with ice. Shake. Strain into a chilled cocktail glass and serve.

METHOD: shake

1⅓oz/4cl cognac
½oz/1½cl Cointreau
½oz/1½cl Chambord liqueur

LOVER'S KISS

Lingering sweet flavors of almond, cherry, and chocolate will make the kiss last and last.

Pour all ingredients except the cream into a shaker with ice. Shake. Strain into a chilled cocktail glass and gently float the cream over a barspoon. Garnish with a sprinkle of chocolate powder and a red maraschino cherry. Serve.

METHOD: shake

1oz/3cl amaretto
½oz/1½cl cherry brandy
½oz/1½cl brown crème de cacao
1oz/3cl fresh cream

Opposite
A 1940 advertisement for the digestif, *anisette.*

MAN COCKTAIL

METHOD: shake

2oz/6cl cognac
1oz/3cl Bénédictine
Dash of fresh lemon
 juice
Dash of Angostura
 bitters

A sweet and sour combination to tempt the taste buds, this is not a drink the faint-hearted. A wonderful spicy *digestif*.

Pour all ingredients into a shaker with ice. Shake. Strain into a chilled cocktail glass.

MIDNIGHT KISS

METHOD: shake

1oz/3cl vodka
½oz/1½cl Kahlua
½oz/1½cl amaretto
½oz/1½cl Malibu

Malibu, a rum-based creamy liqueur with coconut, combines well with the clarity and strength of the vodka and the almond and coffee liqueurs.

Pour all ingredients into a shaker with ice. Shake. Strain into a chilled cocktail glass. Serve one minute before midnight.

MOCHA MINT

METHOD: shake

1oz/3cl Kahlua
1oz/3cl white crème de
 cacao
1oz/3cl white crème de
 menthe

A delicious, minty finish emerges from a combination of coffee and chocolate flavors.

Pour all ingredients into a shaker with ice and shake. Strain into a chilled cocktail glass.

MONKEY SHINE

For everyone who loves the "slip down your throat" quality of Bailey's. The bourbon gives it a kick and the banana adds a light exotic flavor.

Pour all ingredients into a shaker with ice. Shake. Strain into a chilled cocktail glass. Serve with a great deal of monkey business.

METHOD: shake

1oz/3cl bourbon
1oz/3cl crème de banana
1oz/3cl Bailey's Irish Cream

MOONLIGHT

Here is a smooth-tasting, romantic concoction created by one of the Lanesborough's bartenders, Laurent Giraud-Dumas.

Pour the Bacardi, Kahlua, and crème de banana into a mixing glass with ice. Stir. Strain into a chilled cocktail glass. Pour the Mandarine Napoleon and the fresh cream into a shaker with ice. Shake. Float this creamy mixture on top of the Bacardi mixture. Garnish with an elegant chocolate stick. Serve by the light of a silvery moon.

METHOD: stir and shake

1oz/3cl Bacardi rum
½oz/1½cl Kahlua
½oz/1½cl crème de banana
½oz/1½cl Mandarine Napoléon
½oz/1½cl fresh cream

NIGHTCAP COCKTAIL

METHOD: shake

1oz/3cl anisette
1oz/3cl curaçao
1oz/3cl brandy
1 egg yolk

A smooth 1930s classic with a creamy flavor. A mouth-watering combination guaranteed to settle the senses.

Pour all ingredients into a shaker with ice. Shake. Strain into a chilled cocktail glass.

NUTTY PROFESSOR

METHOD: shake

1oz/3cl Grand Marnier
1oz/3cl frangelica
1oz/3cl Bailey's Irish
  Cream

Opposite
Left, Moonlight; right, Midnight Temptation.

A delicious drink with the nuttiness of wild hazelnuts from the frangelica combining well with the orange brandy flavor of the Grand Marnier and the smoothness of the Bailey's.

Pour all ingredients into a shaker with ice. Shake. Strain into a chilled cocktail glass.

OH, MY GOSH

METHOD: stir

1oz/3cl amaretto
1oz/3cl peach
  schnapps

This is deliciously sweet and powerful and not related to the drink below.

Pour all ingredients into a mixing glass with ice and stir. Strain into a liqueur glass.

O R G A S M

An amusing female friend has three levels of excellence that she applies to something. The third level is "wonderful," the second is "to die for," and the third is "it is better than an orgasm." This drink is dedicated to her—and to the young lady who came to the bar and asked me for an Orgasm. She was serious and I discovered this drink.

Pour all ingredients into a shaker with ice. Shake. Strain into a chilled cocktail glass. Serve at the right moment.

METHOD: shake

1oz/3cl Bailey's Irish Cream
1oz/3cl Cointreau
1oz/3cl fresh cream

P E P P E R M I N T   T W I S T

Come on, baby, let's sip the twist.

Pour all ingredients into a blender with ice. Blend for ten seconds. Strain into a large wine glass. Garnish with a small sprig of fresh mint on the lip of the glass.

METHOD: blender

1oz/3cl peppermint schnapps
1oz/3cl white crème de cacao
3 scoops of vanilla ice cream

Opposite
Left, Perfect Love;
right, Green Dragon.

P E R F E C T   L O V E

METHOD: build

2oz/6cl vodka
½oz/1½cl Marie
   Brizard parfait
   amour liqueur
½oz/1½cl maraschino

Opposite
Left, Rusty Nail;
right, Port Flip

They say it exists and this drink must surely be one way to test its ability to withstand the hungover state. This drink is a beautiful pale purple color.

Pour the vodka into an old-fashioned glass with ice and add each liqueur. Stir. Garnish with a fine spiral twist of lemon on the lip of the glass. Serve with a stirrer.

P O R T   F L I P

METHOD: shake

1⅓oz/4cl ruby port
⅔oz/2cl brandy
1 egg yolk

This is my friend bartender Dale de Groff's favorite drink. It gives him the strength to carry on partying.

Pour all ingredients into a shaker with ice. Shake. Strain into a port glass. Garnish with a dusting of fresh nutmeg.

R E D   S N A P P E R

METHOD: shake

1oz/3cl Galliano
1oz/3cl white rum
1oz/3cl fresh cream
Dash of grenadine

A wonderful golden red color and a hint of spice makes this a tempting after-dinner drink.

Pour all ingredients into a shaker with ice. Shake. Strain into a chilled cocktail glass and serve.

RATTLESNAKE

METHOD: layer

1oz/3cl Kahlua
1oz/3cl white crème de cacao
1oz/3cl Bailey's Irish Cream

A superbly layered work of art that's named after the King of the Desert—beautiful to look at, sweet, and powerful, but lethal!

Pour the Kahlua into a liqueur glass then, over a barspoon, pour the crème de cacao and the Bailey's. Serve carefully.

ROAD RUNNER

METHOD: shake

1½oz/4cl vodka
⅔oz/2cl amaretto
⅔oz/2cl coconut cream

A good *digestif* with an almond and coconut finish. Beep beep!

Pour all ingredients into a shaker with ice. Shake. Strain into a chilled cocktail glass. Garnish with a Cape gooseberry and a dusting of nutmeg.

Opposite
A poster for the Italian liqueur, Mandarinetto.

RUSTY NAIL

METHOD: build

1¾oz/4cl Scotch whisky
1oz/3cl Drambuie

A popular drink with a wonderful russet color. It's warm and inviting, like Highland people.

Pour the whisky into an old-fashioned glass with ice, and add the Drambuie. Stir. Garnish with a fine twist of lemon.

RUSSIAN BEAR

METHOD: shake

1oz/3cl vodka
⅔oz/2cl brown crème
    de cacao
1oz/3cl fresh cream

A big and bold drink to make you soft
and cuddly after dinner.

*Pour the ingredients into a shaker with ice.
Shake. Strain into a chilled cocktail glass.*

SCREAMING ORGASM

METHOD: shake

⅔oz/2cl vodka
⅔oz/2cl Kahlua
⅔oz/2cl amaretto
⅔oz/2cl Bailey's Irish
    cream

We've had one Orgasm—here's the
ultimate.

*Pour the ingredients into a shaker with
ice. Shake. Strain into an old-fashioned
glass with ice.*

SICILIAN KISS

METHOD: shake

1¾oz/4cl Southern
    Comfort
1oz/3cl amaretto
⅔oz/2cl fresh cream

For some this is the kiss of death—for
most, a smooth and creamy nightcap
with a hint of peach and almond.

*Pour all ingredients into a shaker with ice.
Shake. Strain into a chilled cocktail glass.*

SOMBRERO

This is also called a King Alfonse in some countries.

Pour the Kahlua into an old-fashioned glass with ice. Gently float the cream on top. Serve with a stirrer.

METHOD: build

2oz/6cl Kahlua
1oz/3cl fresh cream

STINGER

A fine drink correctly served shaken and straight-up in a cocktail glass as it has been served since Prohibition days. However, today people seem to prefer to drink it on the rocks in an old-fashioned glass.

Pour the brandy over ice directly in an old-fashioned glass and then add the crème de menthe. Stir. Serve with a stirrer.

METHOD: build

1½oz/4cl brandy
¾oz/2cl white crème
   de menthe

Velvet Hammer

METHOD: shake

1oz/3cl Tia Maria
1oz/3cl Cointreau
1oz/3cl fresh cream

This is a recipe that I have known since my childhood. The Tia Maria gives it a spicy, coffee/rum flavor, with an orange and creamy finish that comes from the Cointreau. Following is another recipe, which has different ingredients and is called a Velvet Hammer in the U.S.

Pour all ingredients into a shaker with ice. Shake. Strain into a chilled cocktail glass. Garnish with a fine sprinkling of grated nutmeg.

Velvet Hammer American-style

METHOD: shake

1⅓oz/4cl vodka
⅔oz/2cl brown crème
  de cacao
⅔oz/2cl fresh cream

A lighter *digestif* with a delicious chocolate flavor.

Pour all ingredients into a shaker with ice. Shake. Strain into a chilled cocktail glass.

VODKA STINGER

A popular vodka *digestif* with a peppermint finish.

Pour the vodka into an old-fashioned glass with ice add the crème de menthe. Stir. Serve with a stirrer.

METHOD: build

1½oz/4cl vodka
¾oz/2cl white crème de menthe

WHITE RUSSIAN

An excellent after-dinner drink with a coffee cream finish. Great for those chilly nights.

Pour the vodka into an old-fashioned glass with ice and add the Kahlua. Stir. Float the cream on top. Serve with a stylish stirrer.

METHOD: build

1½oz/4cl vodka
⅔oz/2cl Kahlua
⅔oz/2cl fresh cream

YELLOW PARROT

A 1930s classic drink with an apricot flavor and a spicy anise finish.

Pour all ingredients into a shaker with ice. Shake. Strain into a chilled cocktail glass.

METHOD: shake

1oz/3cl yellow Chartreuse
1oz/3cl apricot brandy
⅔oz/2cl anisette

SALVATORE'S CREATIONS

The following recipes have been mixed especially for this book. Each has a balance of aroma, taste, and visual appeal making them perfect for sipping after dinner. A choice of chocolate, coffee, almond, apricot, and peppermint flavors is yours.

CUPID'S CORNER

METHOD: shake

1oz/3cl cognac
1oz/3cl Chambord
liqueur
1oz/3cl fresh cream
Dash of grenadine

Named after an alcove in the Library Bar at The Lanesborough, hidden from view. It's so romantic that couples forget they are in a public place and, if they are very enamored of each other, it can be embarrassing! I raise my glass to all who have cuddled in it—and to all those who will!

Pour all ingredients into a shaker with ice. Shake. Strain into a chilled cocktail glass. Garnish with a small drop of cream in the center of the drink. With a cocktail stick, gently make the outline shape of a heart. Try this once or twice before serving to friends. It is easy! Practice makes perfect.

Opposite
Cupid's Corner.

CHOCOLATE AFFAIR

METHOD: shake

1oz/3cl chocolate
 liqueur
½oz/1½cl Tia Maria
½oz/1½cl cognac
½oz/1½cl amaretto
½oz/1½cl fresh cream

An intriguing combination of flavors that makes you want to lick your lips. Chocolate, almond, and coffee flavors and the kick of the cognac are bound together by the cream.

Pour all ingredients into a shaker with ice. Shake. Strain into a chilled cocktail glass. Garnish with a thin chocolate stick.

GALLOPING GASP

METHOD: stir

1oz/3cl cognac
⅔oz/2cl ruby port
⅔oz/2cl Cointreau
¼oz/1cl anisette

This one certainly makes you catch your breath in admiration for the brilliant combination of flavors present in one mouthful. The result is an intriguing, light ruby red drink.

Pour all ingredients into a mixing glass with ice. Stir. Strain into a chilled cocktail glass.

HONEYPIE

Dedicated to one of my guests who used to greet me with *"Hi, honeypie."*

Pour the rum and cognac into a mixing glass filled with ice. Stir. Strain into a chilled cocktail glass. Shake the cream and honey sharply in a shaker with ice. This will blend the honey with the cream. Float this mixture over a barspoon on top of the rum and cognac mixture. Squeeze a twist of orange zest (zest down-facing) to let a tear drop of orange flavor into the drink. Garnish with a Cape gooseberry on the side of the glass.

METHOD: stir and shake

1oz/3cl white rum
1oz/3cl cognac
1 small teaspoon liquid
   honey
⅔oz/2cl fresh cream

MIDNIGHT TEMPTATION

It was nearly midnight in the bar and all was quiet. The idea of these flavors together inspired me to create this harmony of apricot liqueur and coffee with port.

Pour the apricot brandy, port, and cream into a shaker with ice. Shake. Strain into a chilled cocktail glass. Gently float the Kahlua on top.

METHOD: shake

1oz/3cl apricot brandy
   liqueur
⅔oz/2cl fresh cream
⅔oz/2cl ruby port
⅔oz/2cl Kahlua

SAL'S SINNER

METHOD: shake and mixing glass

⅔oz/2cl cognac
⅔oz/2cl green crème de menthe
⅔oz/2cl white crème de cacao
⅔oz/2cl fresh cream
2-3 dashes of mild (green) tabasco

Created to bring out the devil in you and spice up the hours between after-dinner and bed. The first taste is the spiciness of mild tabasco, then you taste the strong vanilla flavor of the cognac and cream. Finally, there is the fresh bite of peppermint combined with a hint of chocolate.

Pour the crème de menthe and crème de cacao into a mixing glass with ice. Stir. Strain into a chilled cocktail glass. Then pour the cream and cognac into a shaker with ice. Shake. Float this mixture gently over a barspoon on top of the first mixture. Add 2–3 dashes of mild tabasco on top. Garnish with a slim chocolate mint stick and a sprig of mint on the rim of the glass.

Opposite
Sal's Sinner.

S E D U C T I O N

Flavors straight from the heart of the Caribbean—rum and fraise liqueur—meet the passion of French apple brandy for one almighty after-dinner drink. Who could resist such a simple combination?

Pour all ingredients into a shaker with ice. Shake. Strain into a chilled cocktail glass. Garnish with a fresh strawberry and a sprig of mint on the rim of the glass. Cut away the strawberry stalk and replace it with the sprig of mint.

METHOD: shake

1oz/3cl Calvados
1oz/3cl white rum
½oz/1½cl fraise
  (strawberry) liqueur
½oz/1½cl fresh cream

S P I C E   S E N S A T I O N

A great *digestif* with a wonderful peppery nose with a dry, spicy finish. A humdinger of a drink, with each sip presenting the palate with one amazing taste after another.

Pour all ingredients into a mixing glass with ice. Stir. Strain into a chilled cocktail glass.

METHOD: stir

1oz/3cl cognac
½oz/1½cl yellow
  Chartreuse
½oz/1½cl Bénédictine
½oz/1½cl Cointreau
2-3 dashes Angostura
  bitters

Opposite
*Cognac bottles in the Art
Deco style designed for
Courvoisier by the
artist Erté.*

SWEET SUE

METHOD: mixing glass
and shake

1oz/3cl cognac
½oz/1½cl Kahlua
½oz/1½cl frangelica
½oz/1½cl lemoncello
½oz/1½cl fresh cream

Named after my wife Sue, who is the best after-dinner companion. It's mouth-wateringly exciting.

Pour the cognac, Kahlua, and frangelica into a mixing glass with ice. Stir. Strain into a chilled cocktail glass. Pour the lemoncello and fresh cream into a shaker with ice. Shake. Float this mixture over the cognac mixture. Garnish with thin chocolate shavings.

TITANIC BLUE FIZZ

METHOD: mixing glass

1oz/3cl Galliano
½oz/1½cl Strega
½oz1½cl blue curaçao
1oz/3cl champagne

For all lovers who would like a champagne-based after-dinner drink. This one will tickle your fancy. This is my own witchcraft potion. Visually, it's a very beautiful drink.

Pour the Galliano and Strega into a mixing glass with ice. Stir. Strain into a chilled cocktail glass. In a mixing glass with fresh ice pour the champagne and blue curaçao. Stir and float gently over the previous mixture. Garnish with a thin slice of star fruit set on the rim of the glass.

Opposite
Titanic Blue Fizz.

INDEX

Acknowledgements

I would like to thank my wife, Sue, for her love and patience, and Sterling Publishing for their belief in a good idea, and Lynn Bryan. Thanks also to Geoffrey Gelardi, managing director of The Lanesborough Hotel (part of Rosewood Hotels and Resorts), and to the staff at The Library Bar. To all my good friends in the liquor industry, thanks.

The Publisher would like to thank the Bureau National Interprofessional du Cognac for images, Bernard Hine, Maurice Hennessy, Peter Grey at Whitwhams International Limited, and Mark Hunt at Allied Domecq.

Glasses: Thanks to Selfridges Inc. Glass Department for their assistance; also to Riedel, Christofle, Dartington Crystal, Baccarat, and Lalique. Pages 106, Mimosa by Daum from Harrods; 109, Baccarat; 110, Royal Copenhagen; 117, Orrefors (cocktail) and Christofle; 122, Italian Murano from Selfridges Inc.; 124, Iittala (Stella sherry) and Riedel; 127, Lalique; 130, Dartington Crystal; 134, Riedel (left) and Laliu (right) from Selfridges Inc.; 137, Riedel (left) and Dartington Crystal (right); 141, Atlantis (liqueur) and Christofle (old-fashioned); 147, Orrefors (left) and Dartington Crystal (cocktail); 153, Dartington Crystal (left) and Riedel (cocktail); 154, Carlo Moretti (oval) and Riedel (cocktail); 157, Christofle (old-fashioned) and Riedel (cognac); 165, Cenedese Vetri of Murano; 169, Lalique; 173, Saint-Louis flute.

Photographic credits: Pages 6, 49, 54, 69, 83, 84, 89, 96/97; 118, 148, Mary Evans Picture Library; pages 10, 26, 27, 28, 29, 33, 34, 37 BNIC ; page 41, Martell; pages 44/45, 170, Courvoisier; page 42, Hine; page 46, Sotheby's; page 53, Macallan; 58, 65, 66, Peterson of Dublin; 73, 74, 76, 79, Quinta do Noval; 81, Ramos-Pinto; 86, Illva-Saronno; 94, Bols International; 101, Ramos-Pinto; 159, Illva-Saronno.